THE
TOMBIGBEE RIVER
STEAMBOATS

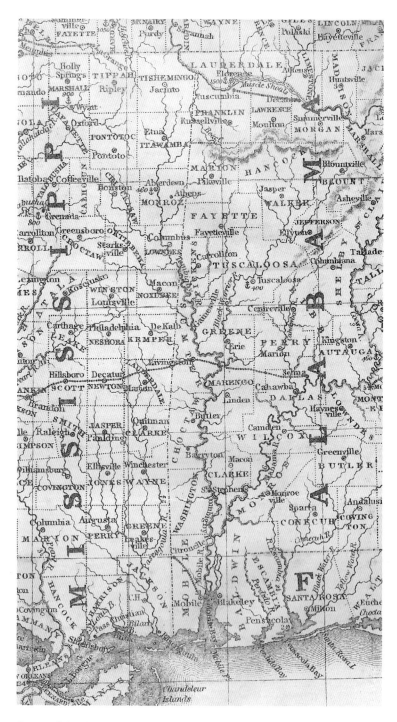

A map of the Tombigbee River Valley in 1852. It shows Aberdeen,
Mississippi, 460 miles above Mobile, as the head of navigation.

THE
TOMBIGBEE RIVER STEAMBOATS

ROLLODORES, DEAD HEADS AND SIDE-WHEELERS

RUFUS WARD

THE
History
PRESS

Published by The History Press
Charleston, SC 29403
www.historypress.net

Copyright © 2010 by Rufus Ward
All rights reserved

All illustrations are from the author's collection and the collection of the Billups-Garth Archives at the Columbus-Lowndes Public Library. Pen and ink drawings are by H. Frank Swords.

First published 2010

Manufactured in the United States
ISBN 978.1.59629.285.7

Ward, Rufus.
The Tombigbee River steamboats : rollodores, dead-heads, and side-wheelers / Rufus Ward.
p. cm.
Includes bibliographical references.
ISBN 978-1-59629-285-7
1. River steamers--Tombigbee River (Miss. and Ala.)--History. 2. River steamers--Tombigbee River (Miss. and Ala.)--History--Pictorial works. 3. Tombigbee River (Miss. and Ala.)--Navigation--History. 4. Tombigbee River (Miss. and Ala.)--Commerce--History. 5. River life--Tombigbee River (Miss. and Ala.)--History. 6. Shipping--Tombigbee River (Miss. and Ala.)--History. 7. Tombigbee River (Miss. and Ala.)--History. 8. Tombigbee River (Miss. and Ala.)--History--Pictorial works. I. Title.
VM624.M7W37 2010
386'.3504409761209034--dc22
2010023006

CONTENTS

ACKNOWLEDGEMENTS

This work is the result of a lifelong interest in the Tombigbee River and its history. I found that the history textbooks of school did little to convey real history and real people. I first discovered the real people of history in the stories that my grandmother, Lenore Hardy Billups, passed on to me. Many of these were stories that she heard growing up during the 1890s. Later in the attic of the Victorian home of my great-aunt, Marcella Billups Richards, I found that she had saved family papers and records going back to the 1830s. I then came across a history of Mississippi written by my great-great-grandfather, Thomas Bailey, in 1853. Those stories and accounts of life in nineteenth-century Mississippi propelled my interest in history. They were the stories of real people. They were people whose lives were anything but ordinary when viewed through a window to the past. As a child, I collected fossils at Plymouth Bluff on the Tombigbee and artifacts in the plowed fields of family farms. Jack Kaye, who instilled in me at an early age the importance of research and documentation, encouraged my interest. History and the act of discovering the reality of the past have always fascinated me.

That interest began to focus on the Tombigbee River and steamboats after first reading and then hearing Katherine Tucker Windom tell the story of the steamer *Eliza Battle*. It was about thirty-five years ago when I first heard the *Eliza Battle*'s haunting story of burning on a freezing, flooded Tombigbee River. Since then, I have canoed, floated and boated the river, all the while researching and collecting photographs and documents related to

A steam boiler washed out of the bank of the Tombigbee near Columbus in 1976.

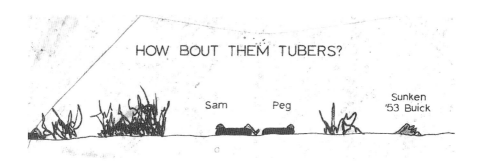

The field notes of the archaeologist from his 1970s trip.

its history. In the years prior to the construction of the Tennessee-Tombigbee Waterway, the winter floods followed by the low water of summer exposed the relics of history. Excursions on the river were always an adventure and a time to see what may have washed out during high water. One such relic was a steam boiler washed out of the riverbank near Columbus in 1976.

The thing about the Tombigbee was that floating down through its history was always fun. One trip in the 1970s even inspired a floating archaeologist to prepare field notes.

A summer day in 1976.

In this history of the Tombigbee, I have tried to make the story of steamboats come alive. Wherever possible, I have used first-person accounts of the boats and life on board them. All of the images I have used are either from the Billups-Garth Archives at the Columbus-Lowndes Public Library or my personal collection, which is located in the library archives.

I must first thank my wife, Karen, for her infinite patience with my collections and the many enjoyable times spent on the river. Debbie Chandler typed up the original manuscript and was actually able to read my handwriting. It is impossible for me to name every person who has helped with my research, but a few stand out for their assistance in research and preparation. Without the help of the following, I never could have accomplished this work: Sam

Kaye, Carolyn Burns, Gary Lancaster, Jack Elliott, Ben Peterson, Mona Vance, Don DePriest and Agnes Zaiontz. West Point artist H. Frank Swords contributed the original pen and ink drawings of steamboats.

I am sure that in the future I will come across additional information that will lead to finding the inevitable errors that always seem to be somewhere in the work of man. My claim to accuracy is that I have tried to use the earliest and best sources of information available. I have made extensive use of nineteenth-century newspapers and magazines in my research. Although they are not always the most accurate account of events, they do provide the best feel for the times and people. This concern for the times and people is important; history that is just presented as a factual statement, without the underlying sense of place, may be accurate, but it does not tell the story. It is the story that makes history interesting.

INTRODUCTION

THE TOMBIGBEE RIVER

The reign of the steamboats on the Upper Tombigbee only lasted about one hundred years. The boats first appeared during the 1820s, and by the 1920s they were gone. With the passing of the years, much colorful history has drifted into the shadows. The chants and songs of the deckhands and the sounds of paddle wheels and calliopes all have disappeared. The colorful language (such as "rollodores," who rolled cotton bales down slides to the decks of boats; "dead heads," the sunken logs that could sink a boat if struck; and "side-wheelers," steamboats whose paddle wheels were located on the sides of the boat) is now forgotten. It was a fascinating part of the history of the Upper Tombigbee River Valley, whose story is worth remembering.

The Tombigbee River flows through the history of Alabama and Mississippi and became the regional artery of commerce and trade. It was known by the Choctaw Indians as "Elome-gabee," or "Box Maker's River," after "a box maker who formerly lived on some of its headwaters," according to an 1805 account.[1] The headwaters of the Tombigbee River rise in extreme northeast Mississippi and flow south, entering Alabama just below Columbus, Mississippi. It then flows south to Demopolis, Alabama, where it is joined by the Black Warrior River. Above Demopolis, the Tombigbee is known as the Little Bigbee or Upper Bigbee. The river continues south from Demopolis to "the Junction," where it merges with the Alabama River to form the Mobile River, which empties into Mobile Bay. The fifty-mile section

The Tombigbee River—probably Plymouth Bluff, near Columbus, in 1903.

from the Junction to Mobile was the favorite racecourse of Tombigbee and Alabama River steamboats during the mid-nineteenth century.

During the winter of 1870–71, the Army Corps of Engineers surveyed the Tombigbee from Columbus to the Junction. The survey showed the distance to be

> *by steamboat measurements 366 miles...Its normal width below the mouth of the Black Warrior is about 300 feet; above, it is 150 feet. It was originally navigable for large boats only in the winter and spring...when it affords from 15 to 40 feet in depth, and the only obstructions were on this stage of water the over hanging trees, which on dark nights and in foggy weather, not infrequently caused serious damage to steam boats.[2]*

High water would normally last from four to seven months. During the low-water period of summer and fall, steamboats could seldom go above Demopolis, which was located 243 river miles above Mobile and 177 river miles below Columbus. The Army Corps of Engineers in 1882 listed seventeen locations between Columbus and Demopolis where the river's low-water depth could be less than two feet prior to improvements made in the early 1870s.[3] Steamboats generally ran on the Upper Tombigbee only

12

The Tombigbee River at Eppes, Alabama, circa 1905.

during high water. During the low-water months of summer and fall, the boats would usually run on the Alabama River.

The first recorded attempt to actually use a mechanical device to propel a boat was by Mr. Duquet in France between 1687 and 1693. Jonathan Hulls took out the first patent for a steamboat in 1736. Hull's project was not completed, though, and J.C. Perrier probably built the first steamboat in 1775, but the engine lacked the power to propel the boat. During the 1780s, John Fitch constructed a steamboat in the United States employing suggestions from Benjamin Franklin. However, his engine was also too weak, and the boat could only obtain a maximum speed of 2.5 knots. In New York, Robert Livingston worked through the 1790s attempting to develop a successful steamboat. In 1803, Livingston joined with Robert Fulton to develop a working steamboat. In the summer of 1807, a boat was completed and made a 120-nautical-mile trip from New York to Albany in thirty-two hours.[4] The era of steamboats in America had begun.

In 1811, the steamer *Orleans* was constructed in Pittsburgh for trade on the Mississippi River. It was 140 feet long and could make about thirty-five miles per day against the current.[5] The first steamboat on the Tombigbee/ Mobile River was the *Alabama*. It was built at St. Stephens in 1818 but was not able to overcome the river's current. In 1819, the steamer *Mobile* reached

13

The steamer *American* at the Tombigbee Landing in Columbus, Mississippi, in 1907 or 1908.

Demopolis but could go no higher against the current.[6] Jean Baptiste Marestier listed two steamboats, the *Mobile* and the *Tensa*, as operating out of Mobile in 1820.

It was the *Cotton Plant* in 1822 or '23 that opened the Upper Tombigbee to steamboat trade. By the mid-1830s, trade on the Upper Tombigbee was beginning to enter its boom years. Over the years, hundreds of different boats carried cotton from north Mississippi and Alabama to Mobile and returned loaded with supplies and merchandise. Almost destroyed by the Civil War, steamboat trade experienced a slight revival during the 1870s but was further hurt by the railroads. However, it appeared to be the construction of all-weather roads and the popular use of motor vehicles that finally killed the steamboat trade on the Tombigbee. It may be more than a coincidence that the first "paved" road in Clay County, Mississippi, was in 1912 and the last large packet boats in the Columbus trade were in 1914. Below Columbus on the Upper Tombigbee, traffic lasted slightly longer, but it also ended by the 1920s.

CHAPTER 1
THE BEGINNINGS

PIROGUES, KEELBOATS AND FLATS

The watercourses of the Tombigbee-Warrior-Alabama-Mobile River Valley have long provided access for transportation and trade throughout what is now Mississippi and Alabama. First Native Americans and later Europeans and frontiersmen traveled along these streams in pirogues, or dugout canoes. By the end of the first decade of the nineteenth century, the need for larger vessels to transport increasing quantities of trade goods and supplies resulted in construction of keelboats. It was not long before the steamboat—which had been refined by John Fitch in 1779 and improved by Robert Fulton in 1807—ushered in a new age of transportation. However, it would be almost twenty years before a general design and configuration was settled on for western steamboats. The first steamboat constructed for use on the Mississippi River was the *Orleans* in 1811. By 1818, two steamboats were under construction at St. Stephens and Blakely in the Alabama Territory. The Blakely boat was "intended to ascend the Bigby several hundred miles above St. Stephens."[1]

The pirogue was for many centuries the means of travel on the Tombigbee. Its use was reported by the Spanish explorer Hernando de Soto when he passed through the Southeast in 1540–43. Through the sixteenth, seventeenth and eighteenth centuries, water travel meant a pirogue. In 1771, British civil engineer Bernard Romans described traveling by pirogue from the headwaters of the Tombigbee to Mobile in his book *A Concise Natural History of East and West Florida*.[2] John Pitchlynn, United States interpreter

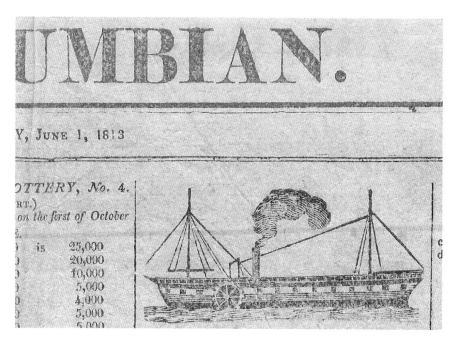

An ad for a steamboat published in the *Columbian*, New York, June 1, 1813.

An 1839 engraving of an early steamboat.

and acting agent for the Choctaw Indians, began using his residence at the mouth of Tibbee Creek (Plymouth Bluff at Columbus, Mississippi) for the storage and shipment of government supplies in 1810. In February 1811, John Kincaid was paid one dollar per day for service "in packing powder and lead from Colbert's Ferry to the mouth of Tibby and boating it thence to St. Stephens."[3]

This larger-scale movement of supplies necessitated a boat larger than a pirogue and resulted in the introduction of flatboats and keelboats. Keelboats and "flats," as flatboats were often called, were both propelled by river current, cable or oars. Flats were designed to transport goods downriver and were rectangular in shape. They had squared ends and a flat bottom and were difficult to return upstream. Therefore, they were generally sold and dismantled when they reached their destination. Keelboats, on the other hand, had a keel and were designed to travel both downstream and upstream.[4]

Timothy Flint in 1824 described the different types of boats in use on western rivers—the West then being the Ohio and Mississippi River Valleys:

A flatboat.

A keelboat.

> *There is the keel-boat, of a long, slender, and elegant form, and generally carrying from fifteen to thirty tons. This boat is formed to be easily propelled over shallow waters in the summer season, and in low stages of the water is still much used, and runs on waters not yet frequented by steam-boats. Next in order are the Kentucky flats, or in the vernacular phrase, "broadhorns," a species of ark very nearly resembling a New England pig-sty. They are fifteen feet wide, and from forty to one hundred feet in length, and carry from twenty to seventy tons...Then there are what people call "covered sleds," or ferry-flats, and Allegany-skiffs, carrying from eight to twelve tons. In another place are pirogues of from two to four tons burthen, hollowed sometimes from one prodigious tree...There are common skiffs, and other small craft, named, from the manner of making them, "dug-outs," and canoes hollowed from smaller trees.*[5]

Documentation on the first boats on the Tombigbee is sketchy at best, but government records do provide some information on early boats. George Gaines had a boat constructed at John Pitchlynn's Tibbee residence in March 1814 to transport Choctaw Factory goods to St. Stephens. The boat was twelve tons burthen, "with oars and cable," and its crew consisted of Gaines and five others.[6] Gaines described the boat in his reminiscences:

I caused the barge to be boxed, as usual in those days. This was meant not only for the safety of the goods but for the protection of the rowers and steersman. I had the sides and top well lined with heavy beef hides, so as to make them entirely bullet-proof. Both ends of the boxing were open, so that the steersman could see how to guide the barge.[7]

In 1818, there was a government arms depot located at Cotton Gin Port on the Upper Tombigbee, which may have required a means of transportation other than pirogue or packhorse. Soldiers constructing a military road from

are plainly obvious—let a Gideon Granger be restored to the head of the General Post-Office, and the mails will be restored to their former punctual certainty in arriving.

A Subscriber.

SHIP NEWS.

PORT OF MOBILE—ENTERED.

Schr. Two Friends, Roberts. New-Orleans,
Sloop Gen. Carrol 'osts,   do.
Schr. M'Donough, —. John, Rum Key,
    Com. Barney, Chapman, New-York,
    Henrietta, Serda, Pensacola,
Sloop Juno, Wright, New-Orleans,
Schr. Susanna, Shepherd,   do.
    Pearl, Edwards, Pearl River.

CLEARED.

Schr. Athenian, Canna, New-Orleans,
    Catharine, Roberts,   do
    Industry, Alvarado,   do.
    Two Friends, Smith,   do.
    Two Friends, Roberts,   do.
Keel-Boat Perseverance, Backwell Claibone,
Schr. Hal, Tansworth, N. York & Philadelphia,
    Esperance, Channings, New-Orleans.

[COMMUNICATION.]

The *Mobile Gazette and Commercial Advertiser* on July 24, 1819, included the keelboat *Perseverance* among the boats entering the Port of Mobile.

Nashville to New Orleans received a shipment of supplies on November 9, 1819, from Mobile at the road's Tombigbee crossing.[8] That crossing point, which had been first settled in late 1817, became the town of Columbus. Cotton Gin Port—where a government cotton gin had been constructed for the Chickasaws in 1801—along with Columbus were the first two commercial centers on the Upper Tombigbee.

Choctaw Indian factor George Gaines also provides the best description of early keelboats in use on the Tombigbee. He had two keelboats constructed at St. Stephens in 1816 to transport supplies on the Lower Tombigbee. The boats are described in the factory records:

> *Young Chaktaw: A barge 28 foot keel, 8 foot 4 inches beam. Timbers cedar and mulberry, bottom plank white oak, side plank cedar, burthen about three tons. Good oars and poles with sockets and hooks. This boat was built for the express purpose of bringing up the treaty goods last fall.*

Deckhands poling a boat on the Tombigbee about 1900.

General Pooshemuttaha: A barge 54 foot Keel and 12 foot 4 inches beam, timbers cedar, mulberry, sassafras, bottom planks white oak, side planks cypress. Neatly covered with planks she is built very flat and draws when loaded about 18 inches water. Her burthen is about 14 tons or 150 barrels merchandise. She is well furnished with oars, socket poles, hooks and jams.[9]

Early local history accounts provide additional information on the development of commercial traffic on the Upper Tombigbee. About 1817, Richard Breckenridge constructed a flatboat at the site of Columbus, loaded his family and effects on it and floated down to Marengo County, Alabama.[10] In late 1819 or early 1820, Thomas Sampson built a keelboat at Columbus. With a crew of two African Americans, he went to Mobile and returned with "family supplies and a small cargo of salt, for sale."[11] Beginning about 1819, Ovid Brown was captain of a keelboat that transported salt, sugar

fortunate there was not considerable more damage done.

The Steam Boat built at Pittsburg, by Roseweldt & Co. for the navigation of the Ohio and Mississippi river, to carry goods and passengers between New-Orleans and the different towns on those rivers, was loading at Pittsburg the beginning of this month, and would sail about the 10th inst. for N. Orleans. We are told she is an excellent well constructed vessel, about 140 feet long, will carry 400 tons of goods, has elegant accommodations for passengers and is every way fitted in great stile. It is supposed that she will go 35 miles a day against the stream, and thereby make a passage from Orleans to Pittsburg in six weeks, but as she must go considerably faster with the current, she will make the passage down in 2 or 3 weeks.
   * There is one way, and one only, by which

An account of the *Orleans* appeared in the *New York Herald* on Wednesday, October 23, 1811. It was the first steamboat to travel on the Mississippi River.

and other supplies from Mobile to Columbus.[12] Gideon Lincecum had moved to the site of Columbus in 1819. There he found an individual by the name of Caldwell who was from Tuscaloosa. Caldwell had a keelboat loaded with a cargo of "Indian goods." Lincecum purchased the boat and cargo and hired the "boat hands" to go to Mobile and bring back a cargo of sugar, coffee and whiskey.[13] On January 5, 1820, a man by the name of Sanders brought the keelboat Cotton Gin Cutter from Cotton Gin Port to Mobile. The Southern Trader, under Captain Brown, arrived in Mobile from Columbus in February 1820, and in 1821, William Viser brought the Columbus Hornet downriver.[14]

On February 25, 1822, the Mayhew Choctaw Indian Mission, which was located west of Columbus and about ten miles up Oktibbeha Creek from the Tombigbee, received more than three hundred bushels of corn by keelboat. It was reported from the mission that "water carriage is of great importance to us in obtaining our heavy supplies."[15] The rule of the keelboat was short-lived, and by the early 1820s, steam power would forever change river navigation. With the great changes that commenced with the advent of steamboats, it is probably fitting that the steamer *Orleans*'s groundbreaking voyage to New Orleans in 1811 experienced the earth-shattering New Madrid earthquake of 1811.

CHAPTER 2
THE FIRST STEAMBOATS

The first steamboat built on the Tombigbee was the *Alabama*, built by the St. Stephens Steamboat Company in 1818. However, it was not powerful enough to ascend the river against the current. A short time later, a three-masted schooner equipped as a steamboat arrived from Philadelphia, but it also had only a brief career before proving unsuccessful against the current.[1] The *Mississippi*, launched at Blakeley on February 2, 1819, was the first steamboat built at Blakeley and the second in the Alabama Territory. It was built for merchants in New Orleans.[2] The spring of 1819 also saw a steamer arrive from Boston—the *Mobile*. In May 1819, it started for Tuscaloosa but, after reaching Demopolis, was unable to ascend the Warrior because of its current.[3] The early boats were a mix of stern-wheel and side-wheel.

By April 1820, the stern-wheel steamboat *Tensa* was advertising in a Mobile paper that it was carrying freight and passengers for Cahaba and Tuscaloosa. It had no pilothouse or cabin such as later boats had. "The Pilot stood on the deck and guided it with a long lever instead of a wheel. It was covered like a shed and could carry about 200 bales of cotton."[4] Then, in May 1820, the steamer *Tombeckbe* was launched at St. Stephens. It was to be completed and running in the Tuscaloosa trade by the fall.[5] The steamboat era in the Mobile River Valley had begun.

Welcome Arnold Green traveled on the Mississippi River steamer *Olive Branch* in June 1823. He provides a good description of an early steamboat, when construction and deck configuration was still evolving:

LAUNCH.—At twelve o'clock this day, the new Steam-Boat TOMBECKBE, built by Messrs. J. H. Dearing & Co. at this place, was launched amid the shouts and huzzas of a large concourse of spectators. She glided beautifully and majestically into the river, without the least accident. This vessel carries about 70 tons burthen, drawing only 15 inches water, and will not exceed 2½ or 3 feet when loaded—85 feet deck, and 17 feet beam. She is intended to ply regularly from New-Orleans to Tuskaloosa, via Mobile, Blakeley, Jackson, St. Stephens, etc. will have accommodations for thirty passengers, and will be completed and furnished with machinery by fall, the season at which the trade of the river will justify her being fitted up. Great praise is due captain J. H. Dearing of this place, for the industry with which he has pushed the building this vessel (the keel having been laid only three months since,) and the multitude of difficulties that must have opposed his progress in the present embarrassing state of affairs. We wish the proprietors that patronage, which their industry and enterprize so richly deserve.   *Halcyon.*

Above: An ad for the steamboat *Tensa* in the *Mobile Gazette and Commercial Advertiser*, April 26, 1820.

Left: The launching of steamboat *Tombeckbe* was reported in the *Mobile Gazette and Commercial Advertiser* on May 31, 1820.

The First Steamboats

A steamboat going up the Mississippi is a curious object and a confused medley. Their hold is used for the stowing of goods, a house built on the deck, nearly the length of the boat, covers the machinery, and the cabin and staterooms for passengers. On the roof of this house or upper deck are accommodated the deck passengers…who here cook, eat, and sleep amidst the smoke of chimnies…About half of this upper deck is a board roof under which as many sleep as can and the balance sleep in open air.[6]

Mobile steamboat traffic began increasing in 1821. The *Halcyon & Tombecbe* of St. Stephens reported on May 26, 1821, that the steamboat *Tombecbe* had arrived from Tuscaloosa and set out for Mobile and Blakeley, that the *Harriet* "passed without calling" and that the *Henderson* had arrived.[7] On October 21, 1821, the *Harriet* was the first steamboat to arrive at Montgomery on the Alabama River.[8] Then, in December 1821, the *Cotton Plant* arrived in Mobile with 330 bales of cotton from Demopolis, Tuscaloosa and the Tombigbee.[9] Only the Upper Tombigbee had not opened for steamboat trade.

The first steamboat that is recorded as overcoming the current and reaching the Upper Tombigbee was the *Cotton Plant*. It reached Columbus in either 1822 or 1823. Built in 1821 in Point Clear, Alabama, the *Cotton Plant* was an eighty-ton stern-wheel steamer with a thirty-horsepower engine. The *Cotton Plant* first became of note when in December 1821 it successfully navigated from Mobile up the Tombigbee and then up the Warrior to Tuscaloosa.

An engraving of an early steamboat printed in 1840.

It carried nine passengers upriver from Mobile and then returned from Tuscaloosa with 330 bales of cotton. The trip took 200 running hours, of which 124 composed the trip upstream.[10]

The *Cotton Plant* then became the first steamboat to navigate the Upper Tombigbee. It arrived in Columbus from Mobile in either 1822 or 1823. In 1824, it reached Cotton Gin Port. Thus it was the *Cotton Plant* that pioneered steamboat traffic on both the Warrior and Upper Tombigbee. Exactly when the *Cotton Plant* arrived in Columbus is in question. Mid-nineteenth-century accounts place the arrival in 1822, but later researchers give the year as 1823. During the late 1840s, Oscar Keeler published an almanac in Columbus. His 1848 edition published a history of Columbus that stated that "the first steamboat that came to Columbus was the *Cotton Plant*, Stephen Chandler, Captain in 1822."[11]

There is another account of the *Cotton Plant*'s first trip to Columbus recorded in the scrapbook of Sarah Neilson. The undated scrapbook contains a quote from a letter written by one of her ancestors. The writer had been a passenger on that early trip and described what had happened. It was stated that the *Cotton Plant* first came to Columbus in late 1822. Its arrival was delayed about two weeks after it grounded on a sandbar about sixty miles

A southern steamboat scene published in 1849.

below Columbus.[12] George Brown came to Columbus in 1821 and, in his autobiography, told of the arrival of the *Cotton Plant* in Columbus in 1822.[13] In a circa 1880 "Historical Sketch of Columbus," written by Reverend George Shaeffer, the 1822 date for the *Cotton Plant* first coming to Columbus is also given.[14] Peter J. Hamilton wrote a history of Mobile in 1898 and in it referred to "her famous trip to Columbus and return to Mobile in 13 days" in 1823.[15] In the 1970s, Aberdeen, Mississippi historian John Rodabough researched Mobile papers while compiling a history of steamboats and found no reference to the *Cotton Plant* arriving in Columbus until 1823.[16] It would appear that the *Cotton Plant* made a trial run to Columbus in 1822 but that commercial traffic did not commence until 1823 and also that in 1824 it made it all the way up to Cotton Gin Port.

Brown's autobiography provided an interesting account of the events surrounding the arrival of the *Cotton Plant* in Columbus:

> *It was in the spring or summer in 1822 that the first steamboat arrived at this place that ever came up the Tombigbee River. The name of it was "Cotton Plant." This created great excitement among the people. Not many of them had seen a steamboat before. We had notice a few days before that a boat was coming, and expectation was on tiptoe. They had a cannon on the boat, which was fired within about a mile of the place to give notice that it was coming. The whole population of the town was assembled on the bank of the river to witness its arrival, and such cheering swinging of hats and waving of handkerchiefs you never saw. The boat stayed two or three days. Someone proposed that we should have an excursion on the boat. This was quickly acceded to. The Captain agreed to carry us five or six miles up the river for $200. That amount was soon made up and, at the appointed time, we all assembled on the boat—ladies and gentlemen—about 200 in number, and had a delightful trip up the river and back, much to the satisfaction of all on board.[17]*

That account is very similar to an account of the steamer *Harriet*'s first trip to Montgomery in 1821. The *Harriet* also took many of Montgomery's citizens on "a pleasure trip upriver."[18] The *Cotton Plant* continued in the Mobile River trade. On April 27, 1822, the *Halcyon & Tombecbe* of St. Stephens reported that the steamboat *Cotton Plant*, Captain Chandler, "had passed a few days

An 1831 waybill from the steamer *Marietta*, which entered the Mobile trade in 1825 and was in the Upper Tombigbee trade in 1831.

earlier." It was headed to Mobile with passengers and a cargo of cotton from upriver.[19] On August 16, 1822, it was the third steamboat that reached Montgomery. As with other early steamboats, the *Cotton Plant* did not have a very long life. On May 7, 1828, it struck a snag and sank at Whites Landing, Tuscaloosa, on the Warrior River.[20]

The 1820s saw several steamboats in the Upper Tombigbee trade. After the *Cotton Plant* showed that the Upper Tombigbee could be navigated, the *Arkansas, Harriet, Balize, Allegheny, Tuscaloosa* and *Herald* soon followed it. The *Bolivar* and *Catawba* were also on the upper part of the river by the late 1820s. During the 1820s, only a few steamers per year reached Columbus. Travel on the early boats was not without dangers. The *Allegheny* snagged and sank near Columbus in 1825. The *Balize* collided with the steamer *Henderson* on the Alabama River in April 1825. In 1827, the *Arkansas* snagged and sank near Mobile, and the *Harriet* burst its boilers at Coffeeville in 1827. The *Cotton Plant*, which had been the first boat in the Upper Tombigbee trade, sank below Tuscaloosa at White's Landing in 1828. Of the other early boats, the *Catawba* was abandoned in 1831, and the *Herald* was lost when it collided with the *Helen McGregor* at Mobile in 1832.[21] Of the seven boats that came to Columbus between 1822 and 1826, five had sunk or exploded by 1828. Even those early boats that escaped accidents had a short life. By 1832, every steamboat that had been in the Upper Tombigbee trade during the mid-1820s was sunk or abandoned.

CHAPTER 3

EVOLUTION OF THE TOMBIGBEE STEAMBOAT

The early steamboats in the Mobile trade were small, often less than 100 tons and usually carrying fewer than 500 bales of cotton. By the mid-1830s, steamers in excess of 150 tons and carrying over 1,500 bales of cotton were in the Mobile trade. At the peak of the Mobile trade, during the 1850s, boats in excess of 300 tons, over two hundred feet long and carrying over 2,000 bales of cotton and almost 100 passengers were common. The Tombigbee steamers were most often built in Jeffersonville and New Albany, Indiana, St. Louis, New Orleans, Mobile, Louisville, Pittsburgh or Cincinnati. However, almost all ports along the river constructed boats at some time. The *Brandish Johnson* was the largest steamer ever in the Aberdeen-Columbus-Mobile trade. It was a 412-ton side-wheel boat built in 1869 at Jeffersonville, Indiana.[1]

By the mid-1830s the configuration of the steamboats followed the same basic pattern on nearly all Tombigbee steamers. The lower deck, with the boat's machinery and cargo, was the "main deck." Above that was the "boiler deck," on which was found the cabin. The deck above the boiler deck was called the "hurricane deck," out of which rose the cabin skylights. On top of the cabin skylight roof was the "Texas deck." The Texas deck had a cabin that housed the boat's officers and, often, a poker room. On top of the Texas deck was the pilothouse.

Most of the early steamboats of the 1820s were stern-wheelers, but by the 1830s, most of the boats were side-wheelers. After the Civil War, stern-

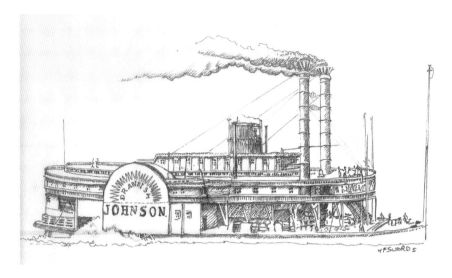

The steamer *Brandish Johnson*.

Pilot House
Texas Deck
Hurricane Deck
Boiler Deck
Main Deck

The deck configuration of a typical side-wheel Tombigbee steamer.

wheelers again became the most popular type. The first steam engines used on the riverboats were low-pressure principal, but they were soon replaced by high-pressure engines. Though not as safe, the high-pressure engine was better suited for the needs of western rivers than low-pressure engines.

The placement of the paddle wheel that propelled the boat caused the steamboats to be referred to as stern-wheelers or side-wheelers. The earliest

The *Selma* was a 320-ton side-wheel steamboat built in 1856 for the Mobile trade.

steamboats consisted of both kinds. The first boats that were stern-wheel were different than later examples. In the early stern-wheelers, the paddle wheel was placed within the lines of the hull. Later stern-wheelers had their paddle wheel placed astern behind the hull. The advantage of a stern-wheel was that it would help push logs and debris to the sides and away from the boat rather than into the side paddle wheels, as was often the case on side-wheelers. When fully loaded, stern-wheel boats drew about six and a half feet of water.[2]

From the late 1830s to the 1860s, side-wheelers were the most popular paddle wheel configuration. By the boom years of Mobile steamer trade, most of the boats were side-wheelers. An advantage of the side-wheelers was that the deck extension, or guards that extended out to the edge of the side wheel, allowed for the carrying of more cargo, and they could be better steered. Side-wheelers not only could carry a heavier cargo but also only drew about four and a half feet of water when loaded. Their average speed was ten to twelve miles per hour. Most steamers had a life span of only about five years. One, however, the *Hard Cash*, survived for thirty-eight years, though it had been almost entirely rebuilt.[3] By the mid-1860s, stern-wheelers had returned in popularity, and soon after side-wheelers became a rarity on the Tombigbee.

Early experiments with high- and low-pressure steam engines and the shape of a steamer's hull were also settled by the late 1820s. Although more

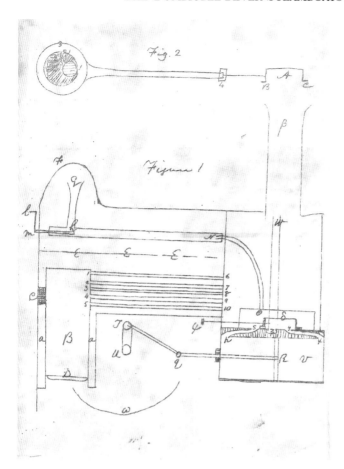

A drawing of a steam boiler created by John Billups while he was a student at the University of Georgia in 1844. Billups would later own an interest in a Tombigbee steamboat.

dangerous and having a potential for deadly explosions, the high-pressure engine became the engine most often used on western steamboats. That was because it was more powerful, lighter, simpler in design and easier to repair. These factors were very important on shallow rivers without repair facilities readily available. Conditions on western rivers such as the Tombigbee necessitated a flat-bottom shallow-draft hull that would "not only draw minimal water but also stem rapids and occasionally deepen channels by plowing through river beds" or sandbars.[4] The steamboat's bow was also often constructed not only to allow deflection of debris in the river but also to allow the boats to be landed on the riverbank.

The engine, boilers and cargo were located on the main deck, and it was there that most of the steamer's physical labor took place. The steamer's

A steamboat engine manufacturer's ad from 1908.

boilers and machinery were located in the center of the boat, with its cargo stacked around the guards (that part of the steamer that extended outward from the hull over the water). This was also where the deckhands and deck passengers stayed.

Under the cabin and boiler deck and in the center of the boat were the machinery and boilers. The chimneys or smokestacks rose in front from the rear of the boilers. Then there were the boilers and other machinery of the boat.

The steamers *City of Mobile* and *Ouachita* photographed in 1905. Their main decks are crowded with cargo.

The boilers on a Mississippi River steamer in 1871.

Those passengers who did not purchase passage in the cabin were placed on the main deck. These were generally the rougher, less refined individuals who found space among the cargo and machinery of the working deck. Here they would fend for themselves and see to their own needs, unlike those who paid for the "luxury" of the cabin.

In 1838, David Stevenson traveled on a steamboat that was typical of those in use on western rivers such as the Tombigbee. The condition of the deck passengers made a real impression on him. He observed that the lower deck, "which is covered in, and occupied by the crew of the vessel and deck passengers, presents a scene of filth and wretchedness that baffles all description."[5]

An 1871 description of Mississippi River deck passengers echoed this earlier description:

> *There we find the furnaces, the engines, the boilers, the kitchen, and the human potpourri, known as deck passengers. Poor whites, Negroes…are stretched, bent and sprawled over boxes, bales, and barrels, some asleep, some smoking, some eating fat meat, and all sweltering in the heat.*[6]

Deck passengers on a steamboat.

It was also on the guards of the main deck that cotton, the economic lifeblood of the river, was transported. Its storage and transport was described aboard the steamer *Fashion* in 1856. Though the description was on the Alabama River, the *Fashion* often was in the Aberdeen-Columbus trade. "The boat [was] stopping at almost every bluff and landing to take on cotton, until it had a freight of nineteen hundred bales, which was built up on the guards, seven or eight tiers in height, until it reached the hurricane deck. The boat was thus brought so deep that its guards were in the water, and the ripple of the river constantly washed over them."[7]

Above the main deck was the boiler deck, on which stood the cabin. The cabin housed what would today be termed the first-class passengers. The

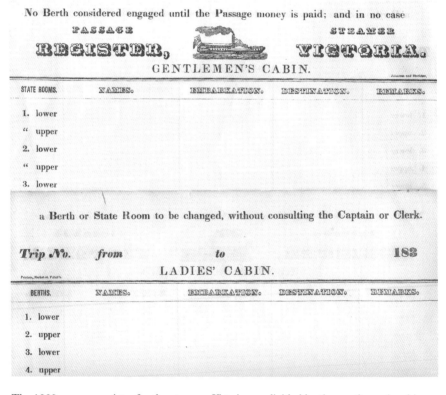

The 1839 passage register for the steamer *Victoria* was divided by the gentlemen's cabin and the ladies' cabin. On the *Victoria*, there were fourteen staterooms in the gentlemen's cabin, with an upper and lower berth in each room. In the ladies' cabin there were eight berths, four upper and four lower. The *Victoria* was in the Tombigbee trade from 1839 to 1855.

Evolution of the Tombigbee Steamboat

Interior of an unidentified steamboat circa 1910, showing passenger staterooms on either side and the ladies' cabin separated by a curtain in the rear.

Interior of an unidentified steamboat circa 1900, showing the cabin's grand saloon.

cabin had a grand saloon in the middle and passenger staterooms on each side. The gentlemen's cabin was located off the grand saloon, with the rear of the cabin closed off by a curtain or door and containing the ladies' cabin. In the front of the cabin on one side is the steamer's office and on the other side the bar. Often the bar would have a side window opening onto the guards to provide a place for deck passengers to purchase a libation. The boiler deck was well painted and comfortable. The cabin would be fashionably decorated with "carpets and contain chandeliers, sofas tables, and chairs… They had fine china, glass, and silver services, every piece having engraved on it the name of the boat."[8] Often the cabin even contained a piano.

Outside of and surrounding the cabin on the boiler deck was a covered area known as the guards. Each of the passenger staterooms would open both into the cabin and onto the guards. When the weather was pleasant, passengers would often gather and socialize on the guards. Here passage was the opposite of that experienced on the main deck.

High above all else was the pilothouse. This was where the pilot reigned supreme, while the steamer was underway. It was usually elegantly furnished,

Cabin passengers gathered on the guards of a Mississippi River steamboat in 1871.

having carpet or oilcloth on the floor and a large sofa. There would also be a cast-iron stove to provide heat during cold weather.

Having many different landings to stop at, speed was very important to a steamer. At first, the boats only ran during the day and would tie up on the riverbank at night. It was not long, however, before packet boats began running day and night and in all weather conditions in order to make as fast a turnaround trip as possible. When traveling through dense fog, it was called "going it blind." A concern was always the chance of suddenly meeting another boat in a narrow channel of the river.

Authur James Wheatly Jr. worked on towboats on the Tombigbee, Warrior, Alabama and Little Tombigbee Rivers, and his father had been a pilot on those rivers. He recalled the way in which boats communicated with one another prior to the introduction of radio. A steamboat's whistle was used to communicate with other boats. The number and duration of blasts of its whistle had different meanings. As a steamboat approached a blind bend in the river, it would blow its whistle to warn other boats of its approach and identify the side of the river it was on. A boat traveling downriver, since it was generally traveling faster with the current, had the preference to pick which side of the river to travel. One blow of the whistle meant that the boat was taking the right-hand side of the river. Two blows meant that the boat was taking the left-hand side.[9]

Nighttime travel required some sort of lighting to prevent accidents. Charles Lanman observed the method used for night travel in 1856. Lanman was traveling by steamer from Mobile to Columbus and described how he observed the crew providing light for the steamer:

> With the efforts of our steamboat hands to make the nightly darkness visible I was amused, for they accomplished their objective by hanging out huge pinewood torches from either side of the boat and whenever she got entangled among the trees which was frequently the case, there was a display of fireworks among the mossy trees more novel than interesting.[10]

CHAPTER 4
THE CREWS

By the mid-nineteenth century, the typical crew of a Mobile River system steamboat consisted of the officers, the cabin crew and the deck crew. In 1871, *Every Saturday* magazine described the crew of a riverboat:

> [The captain's] *business seems principally to be agreeable to the ladies and to such gentlemen as he happens to know. He is like a sovereign in a limited monarchy,—a sort of figurehead of authority, what actual use he otherwise is on board we have not been able to learn. The pilots navigate the boat, the mate commands the "roustabouts," the clerks act as super-cargoes, and the steward rules the waiters in the cabin.*[1]

When the boat was underway, it was the pilot who ruled without question. It was the pilot's job to not only know the river but also every snag or shoal that was in it. There was even a federal law that prohibited anyone from interfering with the pilot when he was navigating a steamer.

The crew's monthly wages varied according to reputation and experience, but usually the officers—consisting of the captain, pilot, clerk, mate, engineer and carpenter—and their assistants ranged from $150 for the captain, pilot and clerk down to less than $75 for the carpenter. The cabin crew consisted of the cook, bartender, steward, their assistants, chambermaids and cabin boys. They were frequently slaves who were leased to or owned by the boat, excepting the cook and bartender, who may or may not have been slaves. The

The captain of a
Mississippi River steamboat
in 1871.

A promissory note in settlement of the pay for the cook on the Tombigbee steamer *Tropic* in 1834.

cook and bartender were considered very important and well compensated or well cared for.[2]

The members of the deck crew were generally Irishmen or slaves, and if they were slaves, they might have been owned by the boat's owner or

The cook on the Mobile trade steamer *Henry J. King* in 1858.

hired out to the steamer by their owners. The deckhands, including slaves, were generally well treated by the captain. The wages of deckhands were generally about $40.00 per month, which would be paid to the owner if they were a slave. Most slaves were even paid "Sunday Wages" of $1.00

Statement of account for the balance owed for the hire of a slave in 1850 by the master of the Tombigbee steamer *Sunny South*.

An 1861 engraving from the *London Illustrated News* of a steamboat clerk recording cotton bales while the mate directs deckhands in the loading of cotton on the Alabama River.

> *1838 Steam Boat Victoria, To*
> *Thomas Thomson Dr*
> *For Labour rendered from the*
> *sixth day June until the 12th day*
> *of may 1839 — making 11 month and*
> *24 day at one hundred and fifty*
> *dollars per month making $ 1775.00*
>
> *Cr: By Cash   1090.00*
> *Bal due 13. May 1839 $ 685.00*

Thomas Thompson's pay of $150 a month on the steamer *Victoria* in 1838 indicates that he served as an officer on the steamer.

Deckhands of a Tombigbee River steamboat in 1915.

45

Deckhands of a Mississippi River steamboat in 1871.

to $1.50, which they were allowed to keep. That was compensation, to a slave, for having to work on a Sunday. Surprisingly, the nonslave deckhands, mostly Irish, were given the most dangerous jobs, as they were considered less valuable.[3]

According to longtime Mobile steamboat captain Owen Finegan, a side-wheel steamer usually had a crew of about thirty to thirty-five deckhands. They did all of the loading and unloading of the boat and were called roustabouts. The main cargo of the boats was cotton. If the river landing was not too steep, the cotton would be rolled onto the deck of the steamer. Where the landing was on a bluff, there was a "slide" down which the cotton would be sent. The crew or "gang" that loaded the cotton was composed of men called "rollodores," who started the cotton down the slide, and men called "stevedores," who received the cotton on the deck and stored it.[4]

F. Law Olmsted in 1856 described the crew of the *Fashion*, a steamer that was often in the Aberdeen-Columbus trade:

Deckhands unloading a barrel of molasses from a Tombigbee steamboat circa 1910.

An 1857 engraving of cotton being loaded on a steamboat either at Prairie Bluff on the Alabama River or Stones Ferry on the Tombigbee River.

The crew of the boat, as I have intimated, was composed partly of Irishmen, and partly of Negroes; the latter were slaves, and were hired of their owners at $40 a month—the same wages paid to the Irishmen. A dollar of their wages was given to the Negroes themselves, for each Sunday they were on the passage. So far as convenient, they were kept at work separate from the white hands; they were also messed separately. On Sunday I observed them dining in a group, on the cotton bales. The food, which was given to them in tubs, from the kitchen, was various and abundant, consisting of bean porridge, bacon, corn bread, ship's biscuit, potatoes, porridge (pudding), and gravy. There was only one knife used, among ten of them; the bacon was cut and torn into shares; splinters of the bone and of firewood were used for forks; the porridge was passed from one to another, and drunk out of the tub; but though excessively dirty and beast-like in their appearance and manners, they were good-natured and jocose as usual.[5]

In 1855 and again in 1857, a Boston pictorial newspaper described and illustrated the loading of cotton onto a steamer at an Alabama landing:

In the left foreground of the picture is seen the bow of a passenger and freight boat, with ladies and gentlemen congregated thickly on the promenade deck, while on the forward part of the lower deck the bales of cotton are rolled on board by a gang of hands. The bales are started from the summit of a high bluff, Two Negroes with cotton hooks attending on each to moderate the speed of the decent and guide them on their way. A large quantity is thus laden in a very brief space of time, when the bell rings and the boat resumes her way.[6]

Where the river landing was located on a high bluff, a cotton slide was often used. Possibly the longest slide was at Claiborne, Alabama. It was described and illustrated in 1855. The cotton was dropped or "dumped down a wooden 'shoot.'" The shoot at Claiborne was nearly three hundred feet long and divided into two sides, one being 365 steps and the other a smooth planking down which cotton bales would slide to the steamer's deck:

When everything is ready below, the signal is given, and the bale is launched from the top. At first it moves slowly, but acquiring impetus as it

The cotton slide at Claiborne on the Alabama River in 1855.

descends, it whizzes down the latter part of the plane, and descends upon the steamboat's deck like a thunderclap, making the vessel shudder from stem to stern. A barricade of three or four bales is erected on deck to meet the descending avalanche.[7]

The deckhands who handled the most dangerous task, such as preventing the cotton that came down a slide from bounding into the river, were often Irishmen. In 1856, Olmsted commented that the labor of Irishmen was cheap, "and they were employed on work where the life of a slave would be in danger, it being cheaper for the Captain to lose an Irish deck hand than one of his slaves." In describing the use of "cotton shoots," he added, "Negro hands were sent to the top of the bank to roll bales to the slide and Irishmen were kept below to remove and store them."[8] A slave, being property, was considered of greater value than an employed Irish laborer.[9]

Captain T.H. Moore of Montgomery recalled the roustabouts as a hardworking "happy-go-lucky" and "irresponsible" group who would often break into a song when working. They had different songs for different jobs.[10]

Deckhands unloading a steamer on the Alabama River about 1910.

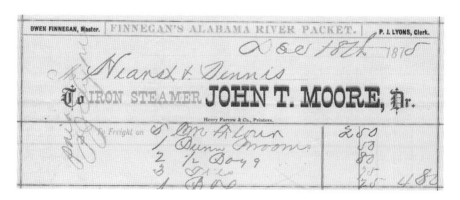

An 1875 Alabama River waybill from the steamer *John T. Moore*.

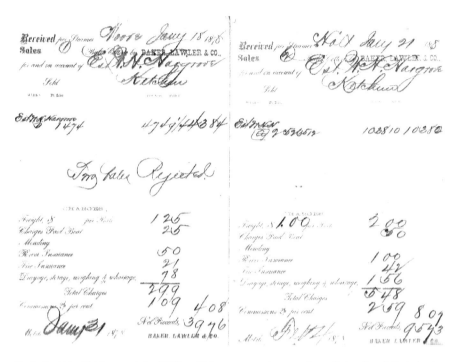

Both the *John T. Moore* and the *William Holt* transported cotton from Columbus, Mississippi, to Mobile during the winter of 1878.

E.R. Hopkins recalled a "deckhand chorus" that he had heard as a young man on the Tombigbee at Columbus. The time of service of the two steamers mentioned dates the chant to the 1870s or 1880s. The chorus went:

> *The William S. Holt and John T. Moore*
> *All them boats are mine.*
> *Oh see the boat go round the bend,*
> *Goodbye my lover, goodbye*
> *Loaded with Columbus men,*
> *Goodbye, my lover, goodbye.*[11]

Another deckhand chant that was recalled from the Alabama River went:

> *Sally is a good gal,*
> *And a bad one, too,*
> *Oh Sally, oh gal.*[12]

Hopkins remembered the many sights and sounds of the steamboats and their crews. He wrote of watching the steamers arrive at Columbus and of sounds that he associated with the boats. "Memory recalls the rough, weird songs, the hoarse commands of the mate, the deep tones of the boat's bell, the hiss of steam and the splash of the paddles as the wheel turned responding to the pilot's signal bell to the engineer." All are sounds that have now been lost forever.[13]

CHAPTER 5

FLOATING PALACES

The removal of the Choctaw and Chickasaw Indians during the 1830s resulted in a population explosion in the Tombigbee River Valley. All along the Upper Tombigbee, existing towns rapidly grew in population, and new towns developed to handle the increased commerce. There were Forkland, Gainesville, Warsaw, Vienna, Memphis and Pickensville in Alabama and Columbus, and West Port, Plymouth, Colbert, Hamilton, Martins Bluff, Aberdeen, Cotton Gin Port and Camargo in Mississippi. In addition to river towns, small landings developed along the river to provide fuel for the steamboats and serve as shipping points for area farms.

Occasional steamboat traffic became regularly scheduled steamboat trade with Mobile. The steamboats operating on an advertised schedule between different towns and carrying both cargo and passengers were called "packet boats." Those boats that only carried passengers and mail were called "dispatch boats." The boom years of the Tombigbee had begun, and by the 1835–36 season, sixteen steamboats were in the Upper Tombigbee–Mobile trade. The larger steamboats that were in use were often referred to as "floating palaces."

Through the 1840s, river trade continued to flourish without competition. Many different steamboats ran from Mobile to the Upper Tombigbee. The steamboat register for the 1850–51 season in Columbus lists thirteen different steamboats making a total of 105 trips. Among these boats was the *Jenny Lind*. It made nineteen trips to Columbus during that season, including

Coffeeville Landing on the lower Tombigbee River in 1885.

A steamboat unloading goods at a small Alabama landing about 1910.

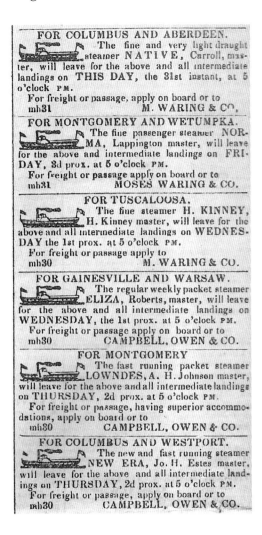

Steamboat ads from the *Mobile Register* in 1846.

one on February 21, 1851.[1] On that trip, the Tombigbee was flooded, and the boat proceeded a mile above Columbus to the West Port Landing. There it loaded 1,100 bales of cotton for shipment to Mobile. That was the largest shipment at one time from a single warehouse on the Upper Tombigbee.[2]

It was cotton that fueled the Tombigbee Valley economy, and it was steamboats that transported it to market in Mobile. Wharfs, cotton warehouses and associated businesses sprang up all along the Tombigbee. Mobile became a center of international trade. Ships arrived from Liverpool, England; Havre, France; Glasgow, Scotland; New York; Boston; and

Galveston, bringing manufactured goods, and returned carrying Mississippi and Alabama cotton. The mid-1840s to mid-1850s became the golden age of Tombigbee River traffic.

In addition to transporting cotton to Mobile, the steamers returned upriver carrying a wide range of cargo. The seaport at Mobile provided an opening to the world, and the products carried by steamer up the Tombigbee reflected that international trade. There was champagne from France, cigars from Cuba, salt from Liverpool and fruits from the tropics. Stores in Columbus and Aberdeen advertised the arrival of dry goods and the latest Paris fashions. During the winter, ships from northern ports would use ice as ballast and sell it in Mobile. Steamboats would then carry the ice to upriver ports. At Columbus, James Blair built an icehouse with thick brick walls on the river to store ice brought up by steamer. Among the most popular items

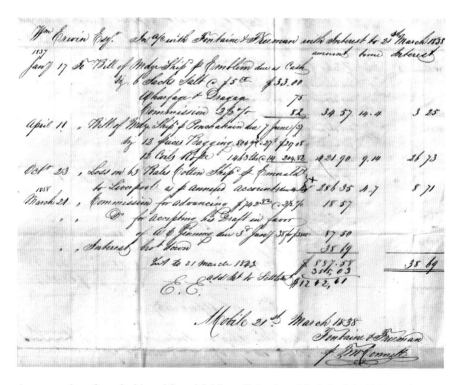

An accounting of goods shipped from Mobile to Columbus, Mississippi, in 1837 on the steamers *Emblem*, *Ponchatrain* and *Emerald*. In return, cotton was carried back to Mobile for shipment to Liverpool.

Ship ads from the *Mobile Register* in 1846.

the boats brought to Columbus and Aberdeen were oysters. When in season, oysters on the half-shell were a popular item on local menus. In Columbus, the large number of resulting oyster shells were used to fill up mudholes in city streets.[3] The Mobile trade provided river towns with luxuries they could not otherwise obtain.

Sir Charles Lyell traveled on the steamer *Amaranth* and wrote a description of the boat in his book *Second Visit to the United States*, which was published in

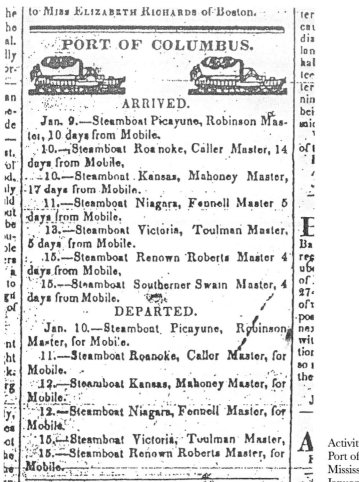

to Miss ELIZABETH RICHARDS of Boston.

PORT OF COLUMBUS.

ARRIVED.

Jan. 9.—Steamboat Picayune, Robinson Master, 10 days from Mobile.

10.—Steamboat Roanoke, Caller Master, 14 days from Mobile,

10.—Steamboat Kansas, Mahoney Master, 17 days from Mobile.

11.—Steamboat Niagara, Fennell Master 5 days from Mobile.

13.—Steamboat Victoria, Toulman Master, 5 days from Mobile.

15.—Steamboat Renown Roberts Master 4 days from Mobile,

15.—Steamboat Southerner Swain Master, 4 days from Mobile.

DEPARTED.

Jan. 10.—Steamboat Picayune, Robinson Master, for Mobile.

11.—Steamboat Roanoke, Caller Master, for Mobile.

12.—Steamboat Kansas, Mahoney Master, for Mobile.

12.—Steamboat Niagara, Fennell Master, for Mobile.

15.—Steamboat Victoria, Toulman Master,

15.—Steamboat Renown Roberts Master, for Mobile.

Activity at the Port of Columbus, Mississippi, in January 1841.

1846. Lyell described the *Amaranth* while it was in the Alabama River trade, but at times of high water it often ran on the Tombigbee. It was common practice for steamers to run on the Upper Tombigbee during the high water of winter and on the Alabama River at other times.[4]

Lyell described his journey on the *Amaranth* in 1846:

> *It was the first of these magnificent southern river boats we had seen, fitted up for the two-fold purpose of carrying as many bales of cotton as can be heaped upon them without their sinking, and taking in as many passengers as can enjoy the luxuries which southern manners and hot climate require,*

A steamboat loaded with "as many cotton bales as could be heaped upon [it] without sinking."

A steamboat loading cotton at an Alabama River landing in 1853.

Sold by J. S. Kellogg & Co.—Booksellers, Mobile.

A steamboat as pictured on an 1840 waybill printed in Mobile.

especially spacious cabins, abundance of fresh air, and protection for the heat of the sun. We afterwards saw many larger steam vessels, and some of them fitted up in finer style, but none which made such an impression of our minds as the Amaranth. A vessel of such dimensions makes a grand appearance on a river so narrow as the Alabama at Montgomery; whereas, if she were a third longer, she would be comparatively insignificant on the Mississippi. The principal cabins run the whole length of the ship on a deck above that on which the machinery is placed, and where the cotton is piled up. This upper deck is chiefly occupied with a handsome saloon, about 200 feet long, the ladies' cabin at one end, opening into it with folding doors. Sofas, rocking chairs, tables and a stove are placed in this room, which is lighted by windows from above. On each side of it is a row of sleeping apartments, each communicating by one door with the saloon, while the other leads out to the guard, as they call it, a long gallery or balcony, covered with a shade or veranda, which passes round the whole boat. The second class, or deck passengers, sleep, where they can on the lower floor, where, besides the engine and the cotton, there are prodigious heaps of wood, which are devoured with marvelous rapidity by the furnace, and are as often restored at the different landings, a set of Negroes being purposely hired for that work.[5]

A Mobile newspaper ad for the steamer *Amaranth* in 1846.

On February 6, 1851, Henry Baylies and his wife took the steamer *Clara* from Mobile to Columbus. The *Clara* was going to Aberdeen with a stop in Columbus. It departed Mobile on February 6 at 2:00 p.m. and arrived in Columbus on February 7 at 4:00 p.m. Baylies kept a journal and recorded his impressions of the trip. Those impressions were later published in the *Dukes County Intelligencer*:

> *The River scenery is exceedingly monotonous & uninteresting. Having viewed half a dozen miles of it one might as well look for interest within the cabin. From Mobile to Columbus, a distance of perhaps 500 miles, I caught glimpses of only one village, Demopolis, & of that only now and then a straggling house. Besides D. there are two or three villages on the River that are concealed from the River by high bluffs. Cane breaks, forests, swamps, limestone banks and an occasional plantation & landing make up all the scenery. The river is principally winding, often turning at almost right angles so that the boat was obliged to stop the machinery to permit turning the corners & then even, she would often almost strike the opposite bank…During the night I became quite alarmed at the snapping & crackling as if the boat was on fire. I sprung out of my berth through the door opening on the outside [of] the boat when my fear was changed into laughter for the crackling*

The steamer *Mary S. Blees* at Demopolis, Alabama, circa 1905.

was of brushes & limbs of trees on the river bank into which the boat
had plunged in the dark. These plunges are frequent & no danger is
feared from them. I was quite amused at sailing through the woods in
a steamboat!

Baylies and his wife returned to Mobile in April aboard the steamer *Cuba*.
The Tombigbee was low, and Baylies described an unpleasant journey. The
Cuba had left Columbus at "rather an unreasonable hour" of 12:30 a.m. on
April 2, 1851. On April 3 at 9:00 p.m., it arrived "through divine protection,
safely at the wharf in Mobile." Baylies wrote:

The river is now very low & the navigation difficult. Scarcely five minutes
pass—not five minutes—pass without some bell jingling as a signal to the
engineers to stop, back or make some change. I rather think the engine has
been stopped on a[n] average every quarter of an hour today to slacken
head-way so as to turn some corner. In on instance, I observed we turned an
angle of about 40 degrees & indeed the river is as sinuous & meandering
as is possible to conceive. Not infrequently we run into the woods in at-
tempting to turn these corners. In some places the tops of the trees are broken
off 20 25 feet above the present water mark—done by the boats during
the freshet. There is often great danger from this…from the branches of

62

the trees penetrating into the state rooms & cabins. Very fortunately for the
boats there are few dangerous snags or rocks & the shores are quite bold.[6]

Steamboats became not only a means of transportation but also social institutions. People often chose the steamer they would travel on by the captain, the cook or the bartender. Speed was another consideration, but it was not so much the time as the reputation as a winner of races with other boats. In 1845, the Mobile-Gainesville packet boat *Eliza* advertised in a Mobile newspaper that

> *the Eliza was expressly built for this trade, has superior accommodations,*
> *her ladies' cabin and state rooms are very large and fitted up with double*
> *bedsteads, expressly for families, and for comfort and speed has no superior.*[7]

In 1850, the Mobile-Columbus packet *Cuba* advertised that Captain Otis's "well known punctually and promptness insured scheduled arrival and departures," while Captain Brainard of the *Clara* thanked "his friends and the public generally" for their "very liberal patronage."[8] When disaster struck, casualty lists that were published in newspapers provided not only the names of prominent citizens who were lost but also the name of the bartenders and cooks who were lost.

An engraving of the St. Louis Wharf at Mobile, published in 1861.

A writer for *Harper's New Monthly Magazine* in 1858 described traveling on the steamer *Henry J. King*, a 409-ton side-wheel steamboat in the Montgomery-Mobile trade. It is a description of a "floating palace" at the height of the Mobile trade:

> *The day following their departure from Montgomery our tourist passed most agreeably on board their boat; and certainly no public conveyance in the world can compare either in substantial comfort or luxurious elegance with those of our Southwestern waters. The weary may repose on spring mattresses or cut velvet sofas; the hungry are fed with the richest viands, served with a quiet elegance nowhere equaled but in first-class restaurants of Paris; the ivory key-board of a superb piano tempts the itching fingers of the musical; books there are for the*

A "gentleman's gentleman" on the steamer *Henry J. King* was traveling on the Alabama River in 1858.

studious…To those whose perceptive faculties are too active to permit the enjoyment of parlor amusements, the moving panorama of the river shore offers a varied and attractive feast; while the mixed and changing population of their floating world furnishes endless entertainment to the observer of character.[9]

The evening meal of January 4, 1844, on board the *Norma* steaming from Columbus to Aberdeen was also described:

The beauty of the evening, the beauty of the women, rosy wine, sparkling wit, thrilling music…when supper was announced. The door was thrown open, and a scene disclosed that would have gladdened the heart of an Apcüsu. A table, extending half the length of the gentleman's cabin, groaned with the rich array of viands, fruits, and cake…Oysters and wine were prominent on the table.[10]

In 1837, there was a lawsuit brought over nonpayment of supplies for the steamboat *Tropic* purchased in Columbus. The court case provides a listing of the stores purchased for the steamer, thereby giving a glimpse of the fare served passengers:

STORES FOR THE STEAMER *TROPIC* IN THE COLUMBUS-MOBILE TRADE, SPRING OF *1837.*

Potatoes, Rice, Beans, Onions, Ham, Pork, Beef, Dried beef, Beef tongue, Cheese, Flour, Sugar, Oil, Lard, Coffee, Tea, Almonds, Raisins, Figs, Dried apples, Preserves, Pickles, Cod fish, Salmon, Mackerel, Butter, Mustard, Catsup, Bottles of cayenne pepper, Table salt, Pepper, Vinegar, French cordial, Whiskey, Bar soap, Candles.[11]

As with all social institutions, steamboats also had their unsavory side. Writing about steamboat travel on the Tombigbee in 1839, Captain Frederick Marryat was not very complimentary:

The steamboats were soon crowded by gamblers, as such was their ostensible profession, although they were ready for any crime which might offer an

A wealthy passenger on the *Henry J. King* in 1858.

advantage to them and the increase of commerce and constant inpouring of
population daily offer to them some new dupe for their villainy.

On Charles Layman's mid-1850s steamboat passage up the Tombigbee
from Mobile to Columbus, he found no shortage of gamblers on the steamer:

Our supply of Gamblers was unusually large, and the manner in which I
saw a game of cards broken up was quite exciting. The hero of the incident
was a rich planter, who had been swindled out of several hundred dollars
by means of marked cards, and who, having had his suspicions roused,
called for a fresh pack, and when the game commenced, very coolly laid a

loaded pistol on the table and remarked that he would shoot the very first man whom he even suspected of foul play. As a matter of course, he lost no more money on that trip.[12]

The elegance of the boats notwithstanding, the issue of safety was also a major concern of the public. In 1843, the Mobile-Columbus packets *Norma* and *Du Quesne* advertised as "staunch built" and "Evans Safety Valve attached," respectively. The steamer *Champion* advertised in 1853 that it had "boilers 5/16 of an inch in thickness" and that it was unsurpassed for "speed, safety and accommodation."[13] Such advertisements were needed, as the life expectancy of steamboats was not very long. Steamers in the Upper Tombigbee trade were lost in several different ways. The *Iowa*, having left Columbus, burned at Fairfield, and the *Triumph* struck a snag and sank, both occurring in 1837. In 1848, the *H. Kinny* exploded at Wilkins Landing, killing seventeen. There was no loss of life, though, when the *Belle Poule* snagged

A poker game in Columbus, Mississippi, during the 1890s.

Cotton shipped on the *W.H. Gardner* in 1881 from Columbus to Mobile.

and sank at Pickensville in 1846, or when the *Motive* broke up on a sandbar at Barton in 1850. Two lives were lost when in 1856 the *Azile* snagged and sank at Ten Mile Shoals below Columbus.

The most deadly loss of an Upper Tombigbee steamer occurred with the burning of the *Eliza Battle* in 1858. That disaster claimed the lives of at least twenty-nine people. The last major disaster involving a steamer traveling to or from Aberdeen or Columbus was the burning of the *W.H. Gardner* in 1887. The *Gardner* was carrying a shipment of cotton from Columbus when on March 1, 1887, it burned below Gainesville, Alabama, with the loss of twenty-two souls.

CHAPTER 6

THE ELIZA BATTLE

Its loss is called one of the greatest calamities in Alabama history. It is the subject of numerous ghost stories and is listed along with the *Flying Dutchman* and the *Mary Celeste* as a famous "ghost ship."[1] A rock band in New York has taken its name from it and written a song about it. It was the steamboat *Eliza Battle*, which on March 1, 1858, caught fire and burned on a freezing, flooded Tombigbee River while on its way to Mobile. The event horrified people everywhere and received extensive newspaper coverage from New York to New Zealand. However, as with any story told and retold for 150 years, fact and fiction have merged.

The *Eliza Battle* was considered one of the largest and finest steamers ever in the Upper Tombigbee trade. Built in New Albany, Indiana, in 1852, it was a 315-ton side-wheeler capable of carrying more than two thousand bales of cotton.[2] Normally it only drew about five and a half feet of water.[3] Its high regard as a steamer is shown by it being selected in 1854 to greet, with a band on board, former president Fillmore upon his arrival by ocean steamer in Mobile Bay and then transport him and the "Committee of Invitation" to the Mobile wharf.[4]

In 1853, it was in the Upper Tombigbee trade as the Cox, Brainard & Company Warsaw-Mobile packet boat. In 1855–56, it was still in the Upper Tombigbee trade as the weekly Columbus-Mobile packet boat. The *Eliza Battle* in April 1855 was carrying goods upriver when falling water levels caused it to halt its trip and deposit its Columbus-bound cargo in a

The burning of the steamer *Eliza Battle* in 1858.

A waybill from the *Eliza Battle* in 1853.

warehouse at Newport Landing near Stone's Ferry, some sixty river miles below Columbus. That warehouse subsequently burned down, and a lawsuit over the lost goods ensued. George Claudis, the *Eliza Battle*'s pilot, described the incident and discussed river conditions:

I am acquainted with the parties in this suit. My age is forty years—reside in Mobile, Ala. Am a pilot by profession—Have been a Pilot on the Alabama and Tombigbee Rivers for Fifteen years and upwards. I was employed as a Pilot on the Steamer "Eliza Battle" in the month of April 1855—Said Steamer left Mobil on the Eleventh day of April 1855 bound for Columbus, water permitting, and proceeded on her voyage as far as Newport. Said boat proceeded no farther in consequence of there not being a sufficiency of water. Said Boat landed and discharged her Columbus freight at New Port on the Tombigbee River above Vienna & Gainesville when we reached Gainesville, I advised the Captain not to attempt to go any higher, as it was clear to my mind that we could not get to Columbus, but the Captain insisted that we should go as high as we could, and we accordingly proceeded as far as Newport. When we reached Newport, we found it impossible to proceed further than Memphis, which would have been about Twelve miles further by water. But as Memphis was on the opposite side of the River from Columbus, it was upon my suggestion that we should put the goods out at Newport in as much as it was more convenient for the Columbus Merchants as the Road from Columbus to Newport was said to be the best, and it would avoid the risk and expense of crossing the River in a Flat. As to my means of knowledge of the water, I have to say that I have been for many years a Pilot on said River, and it is one of the essential requisites of my profession to know the stage of water at Newport what must be the stage at Columbus, provided there had been no local rise there, and that this was not the case, was evident from the fact that the River was falling at Newport.

Cox, Brainerd & Co. are Steam Boat owners engaged in the navigation of the River. I am not aware that said firm had any other Steamer navigating the Tombigbee River at that time. I do not know all who compose the firm of Cox Brainard & Co. I am not and never was a member of said Firm, or had any interest or ownership of their Boats or any one of them. I was employed as Pilot for the year at a fixed salary. Said Steamer "Eliza Battle" drew at the time we reached Newport about five feet four inches. If any other

A bill of lading for James Blair's goods shipped from Mobile on the *Eliza Battle*.

Boat reached Columbus at that time I am not aware of it. The Steamer "S.S. Prentiss" which is a lighter draft Boat than the "Eliza Battle" passed Newport on the same day we landed and only went as far as Memphis.

The Steamer "Eliza Battle" put out her freight at Newport because there was not a sufficiency of water to reach Columbus. It would have been for her interest to have gone to Columbus, and the Captain was anxious to do so. No Pilot would have attempted if he understood his business. It would have been more profitable for the "Eliza Battle" to have gone to Columbus than to have turned back from Newport. Said Boat would not have gotten up to Columbus with her freight. I do not think.[5]

The cargo that the *Eliza Battle* was carrying had been shipped from New York to James Blair of Columbus, Mississippi. The goods left New York on March 2, 1855, on board the schooner *Montrose* bound for Mobile. By April 11, they had arrived in Mobile and had been loaded on the *Eliza Battle* for shipment to Columbus.[6]

On other trips, the *Eliza Battle* had far more serious problems than low water. On several occasions, it had dodged disaster. In 1854, on a trip downriver to Mobile, it was loaded with cotton bales, which suddenly caught fire. However, being equipped with fire pumps, the crew was able to extinguish the blaze and save the boat.[7] Then on November 20, 1855, it ran aground on Croom's

Bar just below Black Bluff on the Lower Tombigbee. In order to lighten its load, a number of cotton bales were transferred to the steamer *Jenny Belle*. The *Eliza Battle* then continued on to Mobile. The *Belle* then ran aground and transferred the cotton from the *Eliza Battle* to the steamer *Sallie Spann*. As the *Sallie Spann* proceeded to Mobile, it caught fire and burned.[8] The *Eliza Battle*'s luck in avoiding disaster would not always be so good.

Viewing the *Eliza Battle* at the Mobile levee just days before its fateful trip in 1858, Charles Mackay described it as an "elegant steamer, a floating palace."[9] The *Battle* had arrived in Mobile shortly before with cotton and passengers from Columbus, Mississippi, and the Upper Tombigbee. In February 1858, it was the Cox Brainard & Company's weekly packet to the Upper Tombigbee.[10]

Its final journey began in late February 1858. It left Mobile loaded with passengers, dry goods and plantation supplies for Tuscahoma, Moscow, Demopolis, Gainesville, Warsaw, Fairfield, Gainesville, Pickensville and

The steamer *Magnolia* in an 1861 engraving from the *Illustrated London News*. It transported the survivors of the *Eliza Battle* to Mobile and was similar in size and appearance to the *Eliza Battle*.

RIVER LANDINGS ALONG THE *ELIZA BATTLE*'S ROUTE

Landing	River miles above Mobile
Columbus	420
Pickensville	381
Memphis	369
Fairfield	361
Vienna	343
Warsaw	328
Gainesville	315
Jones Bluff	292
Bluff Port	274
Demopolis	242
Moscow	227
Griffin's	216
Kemp's	200
Tompkin's Bluff	197
Tuscahoma	180
Coffeeville	140
St. Stephens	120
Jackson	110
Head of Mobile River	50
Mouth of Tensas River	43
Chastang's Bluff	37
Meaher's Wharf at Mobile	3

It was near Kemp's Landing that the Eliza Battle *was lost. On the map, Kemp's Landing would be on the Tombigbee just below the river bend west of Linden.*

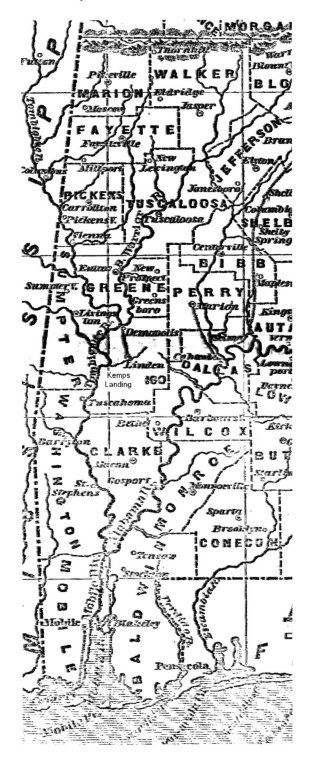

An 1852 map of the
Tombigbee River Valley and
the route of the *Eliza Battle*.

Passage on the *Eliza Battle* for Elizabeth Weir of Columbus, Mississippi, to Tuscohoma Landing on the Tombigbee River. It is dated just ten days before the *Eliza Battle* burned. Tuscohoma Landing was only about ten miles downriver from where the *Eliza Battle* was lost.

Columbus. The weather was warm for February though rainy, and the Tombigbee was rising. It was good weather for a steamer headed to the Upper Tombigbee. High-rising water ensured no trouble with sandbars or shoals and allowed steamers to be fully loaded.

At Columbus, it unloaded the last of its cargo and boarded passengers and cotton for the Mobile market.[11] Its captain was one of the most popular captains on the Tombigbee, S. Graham Stone, and its pilot was the highly respected Daniel Eppes.[12] It left Columbus February 28 and stopped at Pickensville, Fairfield, Warsaw, Gainesville and Demopolis for more passengers and cotton. The *Eliza Battle* was soon steaming south toward Mobile carrying fifty-five to sixty passengers, a crew of about forty-five and 1,400 bales of cotton. It was a popular steamer with a popular captain, and people wanted to travel on it. Twenty-one-year-old Augustus Jones had been unable to board it in Columbus and took a train to Gainesville to catch it to travel to Mobile. Reverend A.M. Newman of Louisville, Kentucky, with his wife and daughter along, probably boarded at Pickensville. Several "relations" of M.J. Clark had traveled to Fairfield to board the *Battle*. "Fortunately they missed it, as the boat was ahead of time when it passed Fairfield."[13] The *Battle* landed at Gainesville Sunday afternoon, where the unlucky Jones boarded it, as a bitter wind began to blow from the northeast, bringing with it thunderstorms and hail.[14]

The balmy weather of the upstream voyage had changed. There was rain, and the quickly rising water became a flood pushing the Tombigbee out of its banks. The almost spring-like temperature became raw and bitter. The *Gainesville Independent* of March 13, 1858, described that fateful night:

> [D]*uring the afternoon a bitter north east wind sprang up, accompanied by occasional storms of hail…* [that night] *the wind increased in violence until it was almost a hurricane.*

Then, according to MacKay, about 10:00 p.m. the north wind blew even more bitter, and the temperature dropped forty degrees in just two hours. The rain showers of earlier turned to sleet. Through these rapidly changing conditions, the *Battle* continued south.[15]

A bitter north wind, described as "almost a gale," was blowing down the river.[16] The cold was so biting that even the stokers who were feeding pine logs into the boiler furnaces could not stay warm. The deck passengers tried to find somewhere warm and comfortable on the open main deck, while the cabin passengers socialized and enjoyed a festive string band playing in the elegant stove-heated cabin. Even those cabin passengers, though, "as they gathered in little groups around the cheering stoves, frequently expressed their pity for the poor men exposed to the pitiless storm without." So intense was the cold that water "spilled upon the deck froze almost immediately [and] large icicles hung on the inside, and oozed through the wood-work of the paddle boxes."[17]

About 1:00 a.m., the steamer *Warrior*, announcing its approach with "a loud shrill whistle," passed the *Battle* "sparking," which meant that sparks were pouring out of its smokestacks. Apparently, some sparks fell on the *Battle*'s cotton bales, setting them on fire. Then about 2:00 a.m. on Monday morning, passengers were roused into the cold by the dreaded cry of "Fire!" Several sources tell of a party or dance going on when the fire was discovered. "Some kind of entertainment was going on on board when it was announced that the boat was on fire. In an instant the wildest excitement reigned." However, the account in the *Gainesville Independent* newspaper shortly after the disaster reported the alarm being spread to sleeping passengers. The paper quoted survivors:

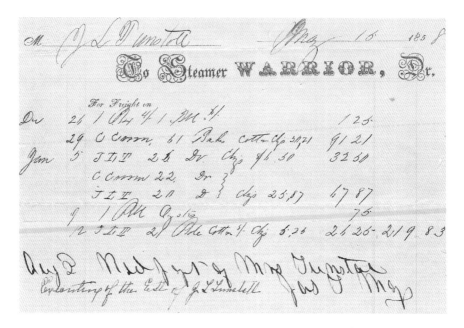

A waybill from the steamer *Warrior*, dated two months after the loss of the *Eliza Battle*.

The cabin door is burst open, and every sleeper starts to his feet, as the word fire, "fire, fire," is shrieked in his ear. "No time to dress-the flames are spreading everywhere. Save yourselves."[18]

At first, the fire was contained to the rear of the boat, but the steamer was traveling south, and an almost gale-force wind was blowing from the north. Fed by the wind, the flames raced forward along the cotton and onto the boat's superstructure. When the flames were first discovered, the pilot steered the *Eliza Battle* for the shore. However, at night with the river flooded, finding a suitable landing place was a difficult task.[19]

The pilot, Daniel Eppes, attempted to steer the boat toward shore, but the best he could do was to run it into the flooded forest by the east bank. Further efforts to control the boat were for naught as the tiller roper burned and all control was lost. The cabin passengers—dressed only in nightclothes and unprepared for the freezing temperatures—were driven from their cabins.[20] There was an attempt made to get the *Battle*'s lifeboat or yawl launched, but it was located aft on the hurricane deck, and all means of access were quickly cut off by the fire.[21] The wind-driven fire forced away those attempting to launch it, and it was soon consumed in flames, as was the aft part of the cabin, which was the ladies' cabin:

> *The passengers were then forced to the forward part of the boat, where every exertion was made to save the lives and property of all on board, but in a very few minutes the entire boat with her cargo of about 1,300 bales of cotton, was enveloped in flames, giving them scarcely time to escape with their lives.*[22]

Realizing the grave situation, Captain Stone ordered the crew and male passengers to "save the women and children first."[23] To their credit, the crew and men of the steamer tried to do just that:

> *As soon as it was ascertained that the yawl and lifeboat could not be reached, as a means of saving the lives of those on board, cotton bales, stage planks and every other available article were thrown overboard, that passengers might cling to them for safety.*[24]

As bad as the flames were, the weather and river were almost as dangerous. In the end, most of those who perished did so not from the fire but from freezing.[25]

The *Gainesville Independent* published an account of the disaster shortly after local survivors and the bodies of the lost had returned to Gainesville:

> *Husbands seize their trembling wives, and mothers their helpless children. With piteous cries for succor, they rush to the fore part of the vessel, and clinging wildly to bales of cotton, trunks, planks, or anything which comes to hand, they cast themselves upon the mercy of the dark, swift stream. Oh! that long, weary, bitter night! How much suffering did its darkness conceal…They had escaped the burning flames, but the cold fetters which the implacable Ice King threw around their hearts could not be broken. God have mercy on the poor sufferers!*[26]

There was one hope other than the freezing river—the trees standing above the floodwaters. As the pilot, helped by wind and current, directed the burning steamer into the trees along the flooded bank, the *Battle*

Burning of Steamer Eliza Battle.

FORTY LIVES LOST!—TWELVE HUNDRED BALES
COTTON LOST.

From the Mobile Advertiser of March 4.

We received intelligence yesterday of a terrible calamity on the Bigbee River—the destruction by fire of the steamer *Eliza Battle*—and, what is worse, a frightful loss of life. It appears that the disaster occurred about 2 o'clock on Monday morning, about a half or three quarters of a mile above Kemp's Landing, when the *Battle*, with some 50 or 60 passengers, and 1,200 or 1,300 bales cotton on board, took fire and was completely consumed. As far as ascertained, thirty-three lives were lost, consisting of the crew and passengers, (about one-half each,) and all the cotton, except some 15 or 20 bales.

Accounts of the loss of the *Eliza Battle* ran on for two days in the *New York Times*.

slammed into a large oak tree, knocking it over. The passengers who before could only choose between the flames and the freezing water suddenly had a third option. People began to cling to the limbs and branches of the trees near where the *Eliza Battle* had drifted. Shortly after lodging in the trees, the flames drove the engineers from their post, and the paddle wheels stopped turning. The loss of power left the boat at the mercy of the wind and river. It swayed around out of the trees in the fast current, and the wind then forced it to the other side of the river. This movement of the boat saved many of those who had sought refuge in the limbs of trees from the flames.

Heroic acts abounded. Jack Jackson (the first mate), Benjamin J. Mitchell (a passenger from Sumter County) and a pilot (probably cub pilot Daniel Hartly) climbed onto floating cotton bales and rode them downstream calling for help. They traveled almost four miles before they were heard and help could be obtained. One deckhand who was a slave had a wooden plank on which he could escape but gave it to a lady rather than using it to save himself.[27] Assistant pilot Thomas Bradley also availed himself of a cotton bale, placed Miss Robinson on it and paddled her to shore. Because of the heat and flames, she threw water on him as he paddled to keep him from burning.[28]

In the midst of the horrors, others also stepped forward. Frank Stone, the nineteen-year-old second clerk and son of Captain Stone, was one of the true heroes. First, he saved a child of Bat Cromwell by swimming to shore with the child. He then returned to the burning boat and "placed Miss Turner on a cotton bale and safely landed her on shore. She said to him, 'You have saved my life; do save my mother, and my sister.' He then swam off and rescued her sister, who afterwards froze to death in his arms. Her mother froze to death on a tree, which was the fate of almost all who perished."[29] After the survivors reached Mobile and told of Frank Stone's heroics, the citizens of Mobile presented him with a gold watch and chain in recognition of his bravery.[30]

Captain Stone found a baby dressed only in nightclothes; he took a blanket coat, soaked it with water and then placed it on burning cotton bales until it was steaming. He then wrapped the baby in it. Stone gave the infant back to its mother and placed both of them on a floating cotton bale. Captain Stone remained on the wreck until the flames had entirely surrounded the boat; he was the last living person on board. He then pushed a stage plank into the river and escaped on it. He remained for eight hours at the scene, rendering all the assistance he could to the unfortunate passengers and crew, and he barely escaped death himself.[31]

Nanafalia Landing on the Tombigbee River, as shown in an 1887 view. This landing was only a few miles downstream from where the *Eliza Battle* burned and sank.

Some of the survivors gave strange credit for the saving of their lives. Among the more unusual stories was one related to Mell Frazer, who in 1909 found that the burning of the *Eliza Battle* was still recalled by people in Alabama: "One person who escaped, afterwards told his experience, and how he sat in the top of a tree all night, and was saved by a plug of tobacco and a flask of whiskey."[32]

Frazer's story probably came from Frank Mauldin of Noxubee County, Mississippi. Mauldin told of climbing into a tree with three others. He credited his survival to drinking a small bottle of brandy and then eating a plug of tobacco as stimulants.[33] In 1951, Mrs. Lillie Borden recalled stories that her mother had told her about the *Eliza Battle*. Mrs. Borden's grandfather, William Stanton, had survived the "ill fated boat," but her great-aunt, Mrs. Henry Turner, and a daughter froze to death. William Stanton had managed to swim to a tree, and his family physician, Dr. S.W. Clanton, made it to a nearby tree. Mrs. Borden recalled:

> *My grandfather, as I told you, was in a tree near his physician, they could talk to each other, and the doctor said he was freezing and my grandfather said he was too. So he told the doctor he had two plugs of tobacco. The doctor told him to chew it and swollow every bit of the juice he did this and lived to tell about his harrowing experience, said next morning they had to prize his foot from the fork of the tree, his limb was almost frozen, had to come home on crutches. The doctor who was with him froze and Grandpa said he heard him when he dropped in the river frozen to death, he was Dr. Clanton. A Dr. Jones who married a first cousin of Mrs. Turner's was lost too…My Grandfather said all through the night he could hear them falling from the trees into the water frozen. My mother was about ten or eleven and she remembered her father coming home on crutches, they didn't know until then if he had been saved.[34]*

The story of Dr. S.W. Clanton was later related in an article published in the *Alabama Medical Journal*. The account told of how, after abandoning the burning steamer,

> *he swam to a tree near by, and secured the safety for the time of a lady friend by fastening her to the limb of a tree, and to protect her removed his coats*

and wrapped them about her. With his suspenders he fastened himself to the limb of a tree where he was resting in the eddy of the high water. When the morning light came and rescuers tried to secure them, both were found frozen to death.[35]

Others also recalled the ordeal of terror that the passengers and crew experienced upon abandoning the burning boat. "The wind was blowing fearfully from the north, and the night was bitter cold."[36] Those who had gotten wet in abandoning the *Eliza Battle* escaped death by fire only to face death by freezing. Charles MacKay provided in 1859 a vivid description that had been told to him of the scenes that followed:

Then a new horror became visible and palpable, and grew more horrible every hour. In this desolate situation, they tend to their women and children, without clothes to shelter them, were exposed to the pitiless breath of a "norther," the coldest wind that blows. Some of them were so weak that strong-handed and kind-hearted men stripped themselves of their under garments to cover their frailer fellow-sufferers, or tied women and children—by stockings, cravats, pocket-handkerchiefs, and other contrivances—to the branches, lest their limbs, benumbed by the cold, should be unable to perform their offices, and they should drop, like lumps of inanimate matter, from the trees into the dismal swamp below.—Hour after hour, until daylight, they remained in this helpless condition, anxiously looking for assistance. They listened to every sound on the water with the faint hope that it might prove to proceed from the paddles of a steam-boat coming to their deliverance, or the splashing oar of a row-boat from some neighboring plantation, whose owner had heard of their calamity and was hastening to the rescue. Even the cry of a water-bird gave them courage, lest the bird perchance might have been startled by an approaching boat; but no boat appeared. There was no help within call. The cold stars shone alone upon their misery. The night wind rustled and shook the dead leaves of last year upon the trees, and the ripple of the river, flowing as calmly to the sea as if human hearts were not breaking, and precious human lives ebbing away upon its dreary banks, were the only sounds audible except their own prayers and lamentations, and the wailing cry of a young child dying in its mother's

Those who had abandoned the *Eliza Battle* escaped death by fire only to face death by freezing.

arms. After a couple of hours, one little baby, frozen to death, dropped from the hands of its young mother, too benumbed to hold it, and, falling into the swamp below, was lost from sight. After another short interval, the mother also fell from the tree into the swamp alongside of her child. A husband, who had tied himself to a tree and held his wife and child close to his bosom, discovered that both wife and child were dead with cold, and kept kissing their lifeless forms for hours, until he, too, felt his hands powerless to hold them, and they dropped from his nerveless grasp into the same cold receptacle. And when morning at last dawned upon their sufferings, it was found by the sad survivors, on counting their numbers, that twenty-eight were missing, and had only escaped the fearful but quick death of fire to perish by the still more fearful, because more lingering, death of cold.[37]

"The deaths resulted principally from the cold. Many of the terrified passengers escaped on cotton bales; some of them were drowned; others swam to the trees, and were found there clinging to the branches, some at the point of death, and others actually frozen stiff."[38] It was a most shocking calamity.

Such were the indelible impressions of horror left by the disaster that, to the present day, families still retain oral traditions about it. Most of these traditions concern family members who lost their lives by freezing after escaping the burning steamer or survivors who had escaped death by tying themselves to trees above the freezing water. Mrs. C.R. Friday of West Point recalls one such family tradition: "A Mr. Dexter of near West Point used his belt to strap a friend to a limb." Dexter and his friend both survived.[39] Oral traditions also survive in the Caradine family of Clay County, Mississippi:

> Bird C. Caradine used to ship cotton down river to Mobile. One time during a storm the boat sank and Bird and his half brother wound up swimming to trees to escape drowning. They were in different trees and could talk to each other during the night. The half brother was never seen again. He had apparently fallen into the river during the night.[40]

The half brother was Thomas Caradine, a passenger on the *Eliza Battle*, who froze to death that night.

Almost four hours passed before small boats could be carried to the scene on wagons and help arrived.[41] At daylight on March 1, several African Americans in a skiff were searching for survivors when their skiff struck the tree in which Frank Mauldin was lodged. Barely conscious, he fell out of the tree into the water, from which he was pulled into the skiff and saved. James Eskridge also directed a skiff through the flooded trees, rescuing survivors. On one cotton bale was found, cold and scared but alive, a small child whose parents were lost. Many of the survivors were found more dead than alive and with their clothing frozen onto them. The rescuers built a large bonfire on the riverbank to warm and revive those nearly frozen before carrying them to nearby homes.[42]

"The residents of that vicinity did every thing in their power to comfort and console the unfortunate sufferers."[43] As survivors were rescued and pulled from overhanging trees they were carried to homes.

Mr. and Mrs. James Bryant, Mr. and Mrs. J. Thompson, Mrs. [R.C.] Pettigrew and others, residing in the neighborhood of where the fatal accident occurred, threw open their houses and placed everything they could command at the disposal of the survivors.[44]

There they were cared for, and large pots of stew were cooked to feed them. The injured were placed on cots throughout the house. One of the injured, Dr. Solomon Clanton, died four days later. In gratitude for their care and assistance, Mrs. Pettigrew and Mrs. R.C. Bryant, who had helped her, were presented with a large inscribed silver pitcher. Mrs. Pettigrew also was presented with two silver goblets with the following inscription:

Gaston Lodge #64 and Citizens to Mrs. Rebecca Pettigrew for Benevolent Care of the Saved and Suffering from the Burning of the Eliza Battle, March 1, 1858.[45]

The bodies that were recovered from the frozen branches and the river were taken to the home of Captain Bryant for identification.[46] The steamer *Magnolia* arrived on the scene about thirty-six hours after the disaster. The *Magnolia* then carried the survivors on to Mobile.[47] New Orleans newspapers reported on March 5:

We learn from a passenger who came down on the Magnolia that in returning thanks to the citizens of the above places, only about twenty-nine were to be found to sign the list, out of fifty-five that were on board.[48]

On March 3, two days after the disaster, the Mobile papers were filled with coverage of what was called the "Terrible Steamboat Disaster" or "The Great Calamity." Twenty-nine people, including fifteen passengers and fourteen crew members, were reported to have had lost their lives. News of the event was spread nationwide by telegraph. The *New York Times* carried a report from telegraph on March 4 and a detailed account, including a list of those lost, on March 12. The *Nelson Examiner* and the *New Zealand Chronicle* even reported the disaster on July 7, 1858.[49] One of

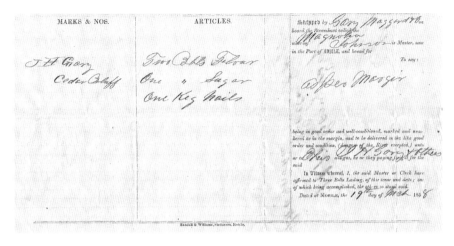

Bill of lading from the steamer *Magnolia*, dated at Cedar Bluff on the Tombigbee River two weeks after the loss of the *Eliza Battle*.

the best accounts was given in the *Daily Picayune* of New Orleans of March 5. It was a summary of the accounts that had appeared in a *Mobile Tribune Extra* on March 3, 1858.

Among the lost was prominent Cumberland Presbyterian minister A.M. Newman of Louisville, Kentucky. Newman, along with his wife and child, was on the *Eliza Battle* traveling to Mobile. When he discovered that the boat was on fire, he pushed a cotton bale into the river and placed his wife and child on it. So as not to overturn the unsteady bale, he jumped into the river alongside the bale. His wife and child were saved, but he froze to death in the frigid water.[50]

After the *Magnolia* arrived in Mobile, Major A.P. Berry formed a committee and called a meeting of the surviving passengers of the *Eliza Battle* to examine the circumstances of the disaster. The committee found that

> the officers of the ill-fated steamer are deserving of the highest commendation for their noble and untiring exertions in behalf of the sufferers, and especially Capt. Stone, the master who, after using every exertion to save the passengers under his charge, was the last man who left the burning wreck.

The Columbus-Aberdeen packet steamer *Champion* carried the remains of victims to Gainesville, Alabama.

Several members of the crew and passengers, including John Jackson, Frank Stone, Benjamin Mitchell and Frank Crawford, cabin boy (servant of Mrs. King), were commended for their "manly and noble conduct."[51] Five days after the disaster, the *Gainesville Independent* reported that the steamer *Champion* arrived from downriver carrying the remains of six or seven victims of the *Eliza Battle*.[52]

There was a follow-up to the meeting of survivors in Mobile, and the board of supervising inspectors made a report to Congress on October 25, 1858:

> *On the night of March 1, 1858, the steamer Eliza Battle was destroyed by fire while on her passage down the Tombigbee River, near Kemp's landing; the boat was loaded with fourteen hundred bales of cotton, and the fire originated at or near the stern, and spread with great rapidity; the water of the river was at a very high stage and inundated the bottom lands, rendering the landing of the boat for the safety of those on board impossible; the pilot ran the boat into the woods; the boat burned to the water's edge; the passengers and crew jumped overboard and attempted to save themselves on bales of cotton. Of the whole number of persons, twenty-nine were lost, fifteen of the passengers and fourteen of the crew; and all perished from exposure to the severe weather during*

the night while hanging to trees or bales of cotton, to which they had resorted for safety.

The life-boat was upon the hurricane deck, and, there being no convenient means of lowering it in time, it was not available, and was of no service whatever in saving the lives of those on board. This is another instance showing the necessity of carrying the boats in such manner that they may be of ready access in case of accident.

A very through investigation was had of this disaster by the local board of inspectors, which resulted in entirely exonerating the officers of the steamer, as they appeared to have exerted themselves in every possible manner for the safety of the passengers and crew.[53]

Captain Stone soon returned to the Tombigbee, and in 1859 he was serving as captain of the steamer *Frank Lyon*. His son, Frank Stone, became a noted Mobile captain in his own right. Shortly after its sinking, the steamer *Wilcox* is reported to have salvaged the *Battle*'s engines.[54] Having been traveling up the Alabama River on the steamer *St. Charles* at the time of the disaster, Charles MacKay recalled not retiring to rest without making sure that a life belt was in his berth and summed up the feelings of the day: "Surely in all the annals of shipwreck there has seldom occurred a more affecting incident than this!"[55]

The story of the *Eliza Battle* took on a life of its own almost as soon as the word of its burning spread. Tales about it grew and changed as time passed. The number of souls lost grew from the twenty-nine to thirty-four, forty, fifty and then to almost one hundred. The *New York Times* gave the toll as thirty-three; the *Gainesville (AL) Intelligence*, thirty-four; and the Congressional report, twenty-nine. Though the steamer had probably left Columbus for Mobile, it was described in a story written in England in 1897 as traveling from St. Louis to New Orleans.[56] Many accounts have the boat leaving for Mobile from Aberdeen at Mardi Gras. It actually set out a week after Mardi Gras, probably from Columbus. The conformation that it probably left from Columbus is the February 18, 1858 waybill from Mrs. Weir of Columbus, which refers to the *Eliza Battle* as the "C.B. & Co's weekly packet"; Doster and Weaver also found no evidence that the steamer went to Aberdeen in 1858.[57]

Although the fire apparently originated with sparks from the passing steamer *Warrior* igniting cotton bales, several different accounts arose of a deathbed confession by a robber. He supposedly set the fire to conceal robberies he had committed on board the steamer. Many of the deaths were attributed to the robber having escaped in the steamer's lifeboat, thus depriving the passengers of that means of escape. Ignored were the accounts by survivors that the lifeboat could not be used because the fire had cut off access to it and it burned with the boat. However, the tales that arose about the *Eliza Battle* do accurately reflect one thing: the absolute horror of what happened.

As terrible as the loss of the *Eliza Battle* was, there were other steamers lost on the Mobile River system with just as great a loss of life but whose names are now forgotten. Part of the reason for the perpetuation of the legend of the *Eliza Battle* is in the frightening circumstances of its loss—by fire on a freezing, flooded river, just such an incident from which legends are made.

No story of disaster as apocalyptic as that of the *Eliza Battle* is complete without a romantic element. This disaster is no exception. Mary Taylor was young, beautiful and the heiress to a large estate in west Alabama. Everyone assumed that she would marry Phillip Saunders, her childhood love. However, that was not the case, for she fell in love with and married another. Saunders graciously accepted his loss though still maintained his affection for the bride. The wedding was in late February 1858, and the entire wedding party, including the rejected Saunders, was to travel to Mobile to attend more festivities. On the morning of February 28, the party boarded the steamer *Eliza Battle* at the Warsaw wharf.

When the *Battle* caught fire, the new bride and groom embraced and leaped together into the swirling river. Both sank, but Mary appeared again on the surface gasping for air. Saunders saw her and dove in, grasping her hand. He swam with her to a tree, where he pulled her up and tied her to a limb. For several days after they were rescued, Mary "lay lingering between life and death." Even after her recovery, she remained in a state of depression over the loss of her husband and would have no part of society or Phillip Saunders.

With the outbreak of the Civil War, Saunders enlisted in the Confederate army. His love for Mary Taylor had never abated, and he had never married.

Warsaw Landing on the Tombigbee, 1922.

He was always found in the thickest of fighting and rose to the rank of colonel. During the Vicksburg campaign, he was seriously wounded while heroically saving the life of another. He was transported home to Alabama, where his recovery was in doubt. It was there that a carriage arrived carrying the lost bride of years past, who had come to return the lifesaving favor of five years earlier.[58]

Credit for modern-day interest in the *Eliza Battle* belongs to Kathryn Tucker Windham and Margaret Gillis Figh and their book, *13 Alabama Ghost and Jeffrey*. Published in 1969, it contained the ghost story of "The Phantom Steamboat of the Tombigbee." That story returned the *Eliza Battle* to popular legend and introduced it to a new generation. Tales about it have become almost apocalyptic.

Today, the remains of the *Eliza Battle* still rest in the waters of the Tombigbee River, though they are not visible. According to William Carlisle of Alabama, "My grandfather was the M&B bridge tender from the 1930s till 1958 and told me that you could see timbers of the boat in the late fall when the water was low…the boat now lies in two sections and…is covered with sand—nothing is visible."[59] Though its remains can no longer be seen, its story lives on whenever tales of southern ghosts or

The site where the *Eliza Battle* burned and sank is just upstream from a present-day commercial barge facility.

"floating palaces" are told. And it is still told by fishermen that on cold, foggy winter nights the ghost of the *Eliza Battle* may be seen steaming down the Tombigbee with its decks ablaze and its passengers and crew eternally crying for help.

CHAPTER 7

WAR TIME AND
THE *ALICE VIVIAN*

The reign of the steamboat on the Upper Tombigbee was brought to an end by dual blows. By 1857, the Mobile and Ohio Railroad had been completed to Lowndes County, Mississippi. The Upper Tombigbee Valley had been connected to Mobile by rail. The 1859–60 season saw nine steamboats making fifty-three trips from Columbus to Mobile. River traffic was half of what it had been nine years before. Then, in 1861, the Civil War erupted. The 1862–63 season saw only six steamboats making ten trips to Columbus and none to Aberdeen.[1] To the dangers of loss by snags, explosions or fire, the Civil War added that of capture. Among the wartime steamers in the Mobile trade the *Swan* was captured in 1862, while the *Alice Vivian, James Battle* and *W.S. Barry* were captured in 1864. The steamer *Lily* sank in May 1863 but was raised and used as a Confederate transport boat. The steamer *Henry J. King* was burned at Montgomery by Union troops in 1865, and the steamer *Dick Keyes* exploded below Demopolis in January 1865. There was a slight revival of river traffic after the war ended, but the great volume of the early 1850s never returned.

During the 1861–62 season, only two boats, the *William S. Barry* and the *Lily*, were left in the Aberdeen trade, and two additional boats, the *James Dellet* and the *Georgia Sykes*, were in the Columbus trade. In 1863, no steamers reached Aberdeen. However, the *Warrior, Cherokee, Gen. Robert E. Lee, William S. Barry, Reindeer* and *Alice Vivian* all reached Columbus. The 1864–65 season saw no commercial steamers reported at either Columbus or Aberdeen.[2] The

A waybill from the steamer *Alice Vivian*, dated 1858.

The bill for goods shipped on the steamer *R.E. Lee* to Moore's Bluff, Lowndes County, Mississippi, in 1863.

dual blows of war and railroads had effectively killed commercial steamboat traffic on the Upper Tombigbee.

Although there were no reported steamboats at Columbus during the 1864–65 season, river traffic did continue. There was still traffic by military steamboats. Many of the former commercial steamboats came under Confederate control and were used as transports. The Columbus-Aberdeen steamer *Cremona* passed to Confederate control in 1861 and was used to transport supplies. In 1864, the Confederate navy intentionally sunk it in Mobile Bay to block the ship channel near Fort Morgan.[3] Among the Tombigbee steamboats that became Confederate transports were the *Lily*, *Cherokee*, *Magnolia*, *Dorrance*, *Waverly* and *Reindeer*.

Military records from 1864–65 provide accounts of steamboat activities on the Upper Tombigbee. O.F. Hamblin of the Second Michigan Calvary was wounded and taken prisoner on October 30, 1864. He was sent to the Confederate military hospital in Columbus, which was known as the "Newsome Hospital." Ten weeks after his capture, he was transported by boat from Columbus to Cahaba, Alabama.[4] In January 1865, a Confederate artillery battery camped at Columbus, Mississippi, was ordered to Columbus, Georgia, by way of Montgomery. The soldiers and guns were to be transported by steamer, while the horses were sent overland. On January 25, the *Lily* left Columbus carrying the troops and guns. Lacking an experienced pilot, it traveled only during daylight. Just below Demopolis, it passed the wreck of the steamer *Dick Keys*, which had blown up a few days earlier killing several persons. On the morning of January 29, the *Lily* arrived in Mobile. There the troops and guns were transferred to the steamer *Reindeer* for passage to Montgomery. While camped near Columbus, Mississippi, the Confederate artillery battery had reported hearing the whistles of steamers in the distance and mentioned the arrival of boats, indicating that the *Lily* was not the only boat hauling troops into or out of Columbus in early 1865.[5] Most river traffic, though, was on the Lower Tombigbee below Demopolis.

All Confederate troops on the Tombigbee had surrendered by April 26, 1865. Three days earlier, the Confederate transport steamboats located on the Tombigbee at Demopolis and described as "the Rebel fleet" surrendered and passed to Union control. The steamers were then dispatched to McIntosh Bluff and directed to transport Union troops to Mobile. The steamers arrived there and loaded troops from the Seventy-seventh Illinois Infantry and two

New York Herald coverage on May 23, 1865, of the surrender of Confederate steamboats on the Tombigbee.

New York artillery batteries on May 9. The "fleet" then departed for Mobile, and the steamboats proceeded downriver, now transporting Union troops, as shown in the order in Table 1.

TABLE 1. MILITARY UNITS AND THE SHIPS THAT CARRIED THEM.

Flagship	*Cherokee*
First Brigade	*St. Nicholas*
	St. Charles
Second Brigade	*Reindeer*
	Admiral
	Dorrance

Twenty-sixth New York Battery	*Jeff Davis*
Third Brigade	*Marengo*
	Sumter
	Waverly
	Watson
Twenty-first New York Battery	*Magnolia*
Pioneers	*Duke*

They reached Mobile in the evening, and at ten o'clock at night they went into camp about three miles out in the direction of Whistler.[6] Also, on May 9, the steamers *Baltic*, *Southern Republic* and *Black Diamond* surrendered to Union forces on the Lower Tombigbee. The steamboats that had been under Confederate control became property of the United States. When they were no longer needed for transporting troops or supplies, they were auctioned off and redocumented to new owners.

The story of the *Alice Vivian* exemplifies this era. Few steamboats anywhere experienced history as did the *Alice Vivian*. It was constructed in New Albany,

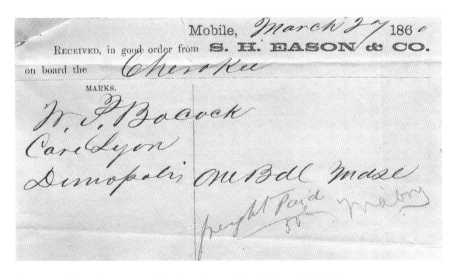

Dray ticket from the steamer *Cherokee* at Demopolis, Alabama, in 1860.

The steamer *St. Nicholas* on the Alabama River, 1858.

Indiana, in 1856 to replace the *Ambassador*, a fast-running Warrior River packet that had burned in 1854. The 376-ton side-wheeler *Vivian* was designed for the Warrior-Tombigbee trade and was named after Alice Vivian, a true belle of the Bigbee Valley. It was the first Mobile steamer to have six boilers and was recorded to have carried cargoes in excess of 2,400 bales of cotton. Judge Fleetwood Foster of Wilcox County, Alabama, described it as "being possessed of a model with sharp beginnings and endings, yet with graceful curves." Foster stated that upon its arrival it was declared "queen of the river."[7]

The 1850s were a time when a steamboat's reputation was often built on speed. The *Alice Vivian* was no exception, and it became famous as a racer. The irony of this is that the *Vivian* was soundly beaten in its most noted race, with the Alabama River steamer *St. Nicholas*. As was often the case on the Mobile River, the race between the *Vivian* and the *Nicholas* was to commence at the Mobile wharf and end at the junction of the Tombigbee and Alabama Rivers. The distance was about fifty miles. The record time was said to have been set by the steamer *Montgomery* in an amazing three hours and ten minutes. Judge Foster was on the *Vivian* during its race with the *Nicholas*:

The start was made amid the greatest excitement—the Alice first and in her wake the St Nicholas. The former so confident of her powers, sounded challenge from her whistle, which was responded to by her admirers on the levee and returned by the passengers and crew. The St. Nicholas always carried a full set of colors—a large streamer from the jack staff. Old Glory from the rear and two smaller one amidships.

As the race progressed Foster further described the scene:

The river was now clouded with smoke, the shades of evening were fast gathering, sparks were flying in every direction, striking the water but to disappear as they mingled with the waves.[8]

The race ended with the *St. Nicholas* arriving at the junction with about a five-mile lead. In other races, the *Vivian* was at least twice victorious over

A steamboat near Jackson, Alabama, circa 1905.

the *St. Charles*, the "twin sister" of the *St. Nicholas*, and also over the *Henry J. King*. During the late 1850s, the *Alice Vivian* operated mostly on the Lower Tombigbee and Warrior Rivers. It was, for a time, the regular Saturday night packet from Mobile to Merriwether's Landing above Eutaw on the Warrior. *Alice Vivian* was also one of the first Mobile steamers to have a calliope. It became famous for playing "Jordan Am A Hard Road" when racing other steamers. Samuel W. Ables was its most noted captain during this period.[9]

River trade was heavily affected by the Civil War, and the story of the *Alice Vivian* mirrors those changes. During the 1862–63 season, it made two trips to Columbus. At Columbus, the Confederate army had established the Briarfield Armory and Arsenal in June 1862. In January 1863, the armory and arsenal was ordered removed to a safer location at Selma, Alabama. On January 22, 1863, the *Mobile Advertiser and Register* reported that the steamboat *Alice Vivian* had arrived in Mobile from Columbus and that its cargo included "a quantity of ordnance."[10] The *Vivian* then went from Mobile to Selma and returned to Mobile. This was apparently part of the movement of the arsenal from Columbus to Selma.

The Civil War, and especially the Union blockade, brought hard times to Mobile. By the spring of 1863, blockade runners were far more

The Alabama River landing at Selma in 1861.

valuable than river packets. Many of Mobile's most noted steamboats were converted to blockade runners. Among them was the *Alice Vivian*. Judge Foster encountered the *Vivian* and the former Montgomery packet the *James Battle* at the Mobile wharf while on furlough from the army in Virginia. He described the two boats:

> [T]*heir hulls braced, strengthened and made stiff to resist the waves—their luxurious cabins entirely removed and in place of their two tall and stately chimneys, there was only one smoke stack to and…their sides walled in so that nothing could be seen.*[11]

The *Alice Vivian* made a successful run to Havana, Cuba, and back to Mobile. It carried cotton to Cuba and returned with coffee, shoes, clothing and medicine.

On August 16, 1863, on a second trip out from Mobile, it was spotted by the U.S. brig *Bohio* and the USS *De Soto*. At about 8:30 a.m., it was captured by the *De Soto*. When captured, the captain of *Vivian* stated that it was from Mobile and bound for Havana with a cargo of cotton. After being seized, the *Vivian* was ordered to Key West. The baggage and passengers of the steamer were searched and questioned. W.M. Walker, captain of the *De Soto*, then reported:

> *Upon examination I find that among these men are several of the staff of General Slaughter CSA. I am informed that General Slaughter had embarked on board the steamer with all his staff, but that a few hours previous to her leaving Mobile Bay he returned to the city, whether the intention of rejoining the steamer I cannot learn, but from the fact that the baggage of Capt. Aldrich and others had been on board it is probable that such had been his intention. The destination of General Slaughter is Texas, whither he was going to raise a brigade.*[12]

The short career of the *Alice Vivian* as a blockade runner had ended.

The U.S. military converted it back to a riverboat. The spring of 1863 found the *Alice Vivian* as a transport on the Mississippi River. It carried the Thirteenth Connecticut Infantry Regiment from New Orleans to Port Hudson on March 25. On April 12, 1864, it ran aground on a sandbar on the Red River. There it had been transporting supplies and three or four hundred horses for U.S. Army during the Red River campaign. Then, in February 1865, it is recorded as helping transport the Seventy-sixth Illinois Regiment from Lake Pontchartrain to Fort Morgan and then to Fort Barrancas near Pensacola.[13] When the Civil War ended, the *Alice Vivian* was sold at public auction. It was redocumented on February 3, 1866, as the steamboat *South*. The times and wear and tear caught up with it, and it was abandoned in Mobile in 1867.[14]

CHAPTER 8

RAILROADS AND REVIVAL

During the late 1860s, there was a revival of steamboat trade in an attempt to compete with the railroads. By 1875, steamers in the Upper Tombigbee trade were going head to head in competing with the railroad and were lowering shipping rates. The lowering of railroad rates coincided with the arrival of boats at Columbus. January 24, 1874, saw the steamers *Planter* and *Maggie Calhoun* loading cotton at the Columbus wharf. The Mobile and Ohio Railroad responded by lowering its shipping charges by $2.00 per bale for cotton. In January 1875, the steamers *Leo, Hale, Lulu D.* and *Maggie C.* were all making regular runs to Columbus. In response, the M&O Railroad lowered its shipping rates to $1.50 per bale of cotton. A Columbus newspaper even suggested that shippers should use the steamboats even after the railroads had reduced rates so that steamers would continue to come to Columbus and provide competition for the railroads.[1] In March 1875, the Mobile and Ohio Railroad responded by hinting that its branch to Columbus could be cut for several reasons, including "the patronage extended the boats."[2] The effort of the steamboats was initially successful, and the late 1860s and the 1870s again saw many boats in the Upper Tombigbee Mobile trade. However, in the end the railroads prevailed, and river traffic never again reached prewar levels.

Some railroads reacted by contracting with steamboats to connect with their railroad rather than going to Mobile. In 1882, the steamboat *Lotus No. 2* ran from Pickensville, Memphis, Vienna and Gainesville to the Great

STONE'S INDEPENDENT LINE

Steamers **LULU D.** and **LOTUS No. 2.**

The Steamer

LULU D.,

J. M. STONE, Master, will leave Mobile every
Tuesday evening; and the Steamer

LOTUS NO. 2,

A. J. STONE, Master, will leave Mobile every
Friday evening for

Pickensville, Moore's Bluff, and Columbus,

and all points on the BIGBEE RIVER during the season. Returning, will leave CO-
LUMBUS and PICKENSVILLE every Monday and Friday.

All Freights consigned direct to J. M.
Stone & Co. will be forwarded free of charges
at Mobile.   J. M. STONE & CO.

RATES OF PASSAGE.

Mobile to Demopolis	$6 00
Mobile to Vienna	7 00
Mobile to Moore's Bluff and Columbus	8 00

RATES OF FREIGHT:

Cotton, per bale	$1 50
Up freight—dry barrels	50
wet barrels	73
Whiskey and Molasses	1 00
Bacon, per hogshead	3 00
Sugar, per hogshead	4 00
Small packages, each	25

Other freights in proportion.
oct24–

Above: The Columbus,
Mississippi riverfront in 1870.

Left: A newspaper ad from
the *Columbus Democrat*,
January 31, 1875, advertising
steamboat rates to Mobile.

Southern Railroad at Demopolis rather than Mobile. One railroad, the Central Railroad and Banking Company of Georgia, even owned the *William S. Holt*, a steamboat on the Tombigbee that ran between Columbus and Demopolis.[3]

The impact of the railroads is evident in two ads for the *Lotus No. 2*. One is from the *Columbus Democrat* of January 31, 1875, advertising rates to Mobile. The other is from the *Columbus Tri-Weekly Index* of January 24, 1883. By 1883, the *Lotus No. 2* connected Columbus with the Alabama Great Southern Railroad and not Mobile.

Although greatly reduced, steamboat traffic did survive on the Upper Tombigbee. Among the steamboats then in the Upper Tombigbee trade were the *Alice M.*, 1865–66; *Billy Collins*, Columbus to the railroad at Miller's Landing, late 1870s; *Emma Lee*; Upper Tombigbee trade, 1870–71;

For PICKENSVILLE, MEMPHIS, VIENNA, GAINESVILLE and MILLER'S LANDING—connecting with the Alabama Great Southern Railroad.

 The A No. 1 first class Freight and Passenger Steamer,

LOTUS No. 2,

JOHN DOYLE, Master........JAS. O. JORDAN, Clerk.

Will leave for the above and all way landing during the present season, making two trips per week, water permitting.

For freight or passage apply on board or to BILLUPS & BANKS, Agents.

Nov. 28, 1882.

A newspaper ad from the *Columbus Tri-Weekly Index*, January 24, 1883, noting that the steamer *Lotus No. 2* connects Columbus with the Alabama Great Southern Railroad rather than Mobile.

FOR MOBILE.

The A No. 1 side-wheel Freight and Passenger Steamer,

"LEO,"

JAS. G. STEWART, Master,

Will commence her weekly trips as above on the first rise of the river, and continue during the season.

The LEO classes A No. 1, in all Insurance companies. A share of the public patronage respectfully solicited.

Through rates given and bill ladings signed to and from New Orleans.

A newspaper ad from the *Columbus Democrat*, January 31, 1875, for the steamer *Leo*.

W.H. Gardner, Upper Tombigbee trade, 1880–87; *Hard Cash*, in the Upper Tombigbee trade, various times from 1876 to 1912; *Hattie B. Moore*, in the Upper Tombigbee trade, 1883; *Lotus No. 2*, in the Upper Tombigbee trade, 1875–82; *Lulu D.* and *Leo*, Upper Tombigbee trade, 1875–76; *Mary Boyd*, Vienna trade, 1882–83; *Mary Conley*, Aberdeen or Columbus trade, 1866–68; *Mist*, Aberdeen-Columbus trade, 1865–67; *R.E. Lee*, Pickensville trade, 1890; *Reindeer*, Columbus trade, 1865–68; *Ruth*, Vienna trade, 1879–83; *Virginia*, 1865–67; and *William S. Holt*, Columbus trade, 1875–77.

A good snapshot of Upper Tombigbee cotton shipping during the late 1870s and early 1880s is found in the estate records of W.H. Hargrove of Lowndes County, Mississippi. Hargrove's estate included a farm near Columbus that sold cotton through cotton factors Baker, Lawler & Company of Mobile, Alabama. The records reflect the use of the Mobile and Ohio Railroad for shipping cotton to Mobile during the fall, when the river was low, and shipping by steamer during the winter high water. The effect of competition between the railroad and steamboats is very apparent in these records. In October 1877, the Mobile and Ohio Railroad was charging $4.00 per bale for freight to ship a bale of cotton to Mobile. However, after the river at Columbus rose sufficiently for steamboats to travel, the steamer *Holt* arrived at Columbus and started shipping cotton for only $1.50 per bale.

Unfortunately, the records are not clear as to whether all of the cotton was going to Mobile or was only going to the railheads at Eppes and Demopolis. The steamer *Holt* was partially owned by the Central Railroad and Banking Company of Georgia and on several occasions made a round trip from Columbus in three days. Such a short trip time would indicate that the *Holt* did not travel all the way to Mobile but only went so far as the railheads at Eppes or Demopolis. What the records do show is the frequency and amount of steamer traffic at Columbus about 1880.

During the 1877–78 season, four different steamboats—*Holt, Lotus No. 2, Moore* and *Johnson*—transported cotton for the Hargrove estate between

A Columbus and Greenville Railway train about to cross the Tombigbee circa 1920.

A box of tobacco shipped on the Central Railroad & Banking Company of Georgia in 1892.

November 10, 1877, and May 14, 1878. The steamers carried estate cotton on sixteen occasions, with eleven of those trips using the *Holt*.

During the 1878–79 season, the estate used four steamboats—the *Lulu D.*, *Fleta*, *Johnson* and *Moore*—to transport cotton. However, between December 6, 1878, and January 27, 1879, cotton was only shipped six times.

The 1879–80 season saw seven different steamers used to transport estate cotton. They were the *Lillie Lou*, *Lulu D.*, *Ruth*, *Lotus No. 2*, *Era*, *Hale* and *Johnson*. The season ran from November 21, 1878, to March 20, 1879, and a total of eleven trips were made, but no single steamer made more than three trips carrying Hargrove cotton.

The last season for which Hargrove records exist is the 1880–81 season, which extended from December 6, 1880, to January 20, 1881. Five boats made a total of six trips. The *Gardner* twice transported Hargrove cotton, and the *Era*, *Johnson*, *Ruth* and *Lotus No. 2* each made one trip.[4]

The Hargrove estate records provide evidence of the interaction of railroads and steamboats along the Tombigbee. There was competition between river traffic and the north–south running of the Mobile and Ohio Railroad. At the same time, east–west railroads, such as the Central Railroad and Banking Company of Georgia, were using steamboats to

The steamer *William S. Holt* was partly owned by the Central Railroad & Banking Company of Georgia and ran on the Upper Tombigbee River.

divert cotton shipments from Mobile to their Tombigbee railhead at Demopolis and thence to Savannah, Georgia. Thus, although the Mobile and Ohio Railroad viewed the river as competition, the Central Railroad and Banking Company of Georgia viewed the river as a means of connecting the hinterlands to its railroad.[5]

One of the biggest obstacles that steamboats faced was having sufficient water depth in the Tombigbee. Before the arrival of the railroads, there was no viable alternative other than waiting for high water to ship cotton. Navigation for large boats was only considered practical when the river stage at Columbus was more than six feet above low water. That resulted in there being only four to seven months out of the year that the Tombigbee was navigable to Columbus or above. Aberdeen required a river stage of twelve feet at Columbus for safe navigation.[6] The photographs here provide a comparison of the river at Aberdeen and Columbus.

In 1871, Congress authorized a project to improve navigation on the Tombigbee from Mobile to Columbus, Mississippi, and on the Warrior River to Tuscaloosa. The original plan called for the removal of snags and the deepening of bars and shoals, including the removal of snags from Ten Mile Shoals, 13.23 miles below Columbus. In 1873, Congress

The Tombigbee River bridge at Aberdeen, Mississippi, circa 1910.

The Tombigbee River bridge at Columbus, Mississippi, circa 1905.

also approved a project to improve river navigation above Columbus at high water. Funds were approved to remove snags, logs and overhanging trees above Columbus. It was soon evident that more extensive work was needed on the channel to improve navigation. In 1878, Congress approved a modified project plan. That modified plan called for improvements in

The Ten Mile Shoals in the Tombigbee River below Columbus in 1922.

the river channel to attain a "4-foot channel of navigable depth from the mouth to Demopolis, and a depth of not less than 3 feet from Demopolis, Alabama to Columbus, Mississippi."[7]

Because of limited funding, most of the work had initially been only about improving the Warrior River. However, in September 1878, the work boats and crews were moved to the Tombigbee. The boats were working up the Tombigbee, and on May 11, 1880, they reached the foot of Ten Mile Shoals below Columbus. Work continued at the shoals until it was stopped by high water on September 1. Because of continued high water, all work stopped on November 9, and the boats were docked at Columbus for the winter. In preparation for low water and renewing the work, the boats were "taken out on a bar and calked" in March 1881.[8]

Work on the Tombigbee below Columbus recommenced on March 20, 1881. By May 23, the Army Corps of Engineers working between Columbus and the head of Ten Mile Shoals was employing a full crew. On July 1, the work crew was under the direction of Assistant H.B. Warren and was composed of "a log boat with a crew of twelve men, and a quarter boat, barge, and campage for twenty-five men." The work included removing logs, cutting overhanging trees, deepening bars and constructing dams and jetties to maintain the work done on bars. From Vienna to Columbus, a river distance of seventy-seven miles, twelve major bars were improved. There had been eleven bars that made up Ten Mile Shoals with a low-water depth as low as fourteen inches. Their minimum depth at low water was increased to two feet eight inches.[9] Between the shoals and Columbus, bars were also deepened at Butler's, Gaston's, Rock Shoals, Huddleston's and Curtis Island. At Rock Shoals, 2.5 miles below Columbus, "a channel 35 feet by 3 feet in depth was blasted."[10] The season's work ended with high water on November 27, 1881. Through their heavy use, the Army Corps of Engineers log-boat and quarter-boat had become unserviceable and were not worth repairing. They were dismantled and sunk into jetties near Vienna.[11]

The Army Corps of Engineers working to improve navigation on the Tombigbee between Columbus and Vienna had removed 5,130 snags, stumps and sunken logs by the late 1880s. In addition, forty-two bars or shoals had been improved, including the infamous Ten Mile Shoals that was composed of at least eleven individual shoals. The result was that the Tombigbee became navigable to Columbus at a river stage of two feet at Columbus, to Aberdeen when the river stage at Columbus was four feet and when at ten feet at Columbus the river was navigable all the way up to Fulton. However, the Army Corps of Engineers determined that only a slack water system of locks and dams would allow year-round navigation to Columbus and Aberdeen.

Improvements were also authorized from the Noxubee River. Because of competition from the Mobile and Ohio Railroad, steamboat traffic up the Noxubee River to Macon was withdrawn after 1856. The Army Corps of Engineers in 1882 reported that after steamer traffic ended "the river banks then became overgrown with timber, which in time fell or slid into the river, causing snags and logs to lodge on the river bottom, and also the formation of shoals and bars." The construction of fish traps in the river channel also caused drifts to form. In 1880, the Army Corps of Engineers was directed to reopen a channel to Macon by removing obstructions. From 1880 to 1881, the organization reported removing twelve fish traps and drifts, 28,404 overhanging trees and 2,857 logs and snags. There were also 5,450 large stumps on the bank cut level and 2,978 logs (drift) on the bank cut up. In 1881, a small steamer made it up forty-five miles of the Noxubee before a heavy drift stopped it. That was the first attempt by a steamboat to reach Macon since about 1856.[12]

With navigation still limited to seasonal high water, steamboats were hard-pressed to compete with the expanding railroads. The boats that did

Steamer *Lotus No. 2* at Mobile in 1892.

continue to run often had ties to railroads. In 1875, the 225-ton, 135-foot by 28-foot stern-wheeler *William S. Holt* was purchased specifically to run between Columbus and the railroad at Demopolis,[13] as was also the steamer *Lotus No. 2* that ran in the 1880s from the Upper Tombigbee to the Great Southern Railroad at Demopolis.

The sixty-ton steamer *Billy Collins* ran from Columbus to the Alabama Great Southern Railroad during the 1881–82 season. It carried 7,010 bales of cotton from Columbus to the railroad. It also carried 1,117 bales of cotton and 6,588 sacks of cottonseed from way landings to Columbus. In addition, about one hundred carloads of other merchandise were carried to Columbus. The competition between the Mobile and Ohio Railroad and the steamboats was stiff. During high water, the railroad only charged a rate of $0.65 cotton per CWT, but in low water the railroad rate increased to $1.20 per CWT cotton.[14]

A view showing Webb's Landing on the Tombigbee River, Demopolis, Alabama, during the spring of 1905. Several pre-1910 postcards show the same scene but are found labeled as either the Columbus or Demopolis landings.

During the 1881–82 season, six steamboats from Mobile and one from Columbus operated on the Upper Tombigbee. They ranged in capacity from 600 to 1,200 bales of cotton. In addition, many timber rafts and flatboats loaded with lumber also floated down the river, including more than 6,000 logs from above Aberdeen. The season's total commerce between Mobile and the Upper Tombigbee included 10,500 passengers, up and down; 32,000 tons of freight such as bacon, flour, cornmeal and groceries; 45,557 bales of cotton; and 82,000 sacks of cottonseed.[15]

The first decade of the twentieth century saw a limited number of boats still operating on the upper part of the river. The glamour was gone, and railroads were the preferred mode of transportation. However, people and communities along the river who lacked access to railroads still depended on steamboats for transportation. Mrs. Ethel Smith Watson, who grew up in Clay County, Mississippi, near the Tombigbee just after the turn of the century, remembered steamboats on the river. In a 1980 interview, she recalled traveling on the steamer *Hard Cash* as a child:

The steamer *Hard Cash* at the Mobile Wharf, circa 1908.

They had little berths in which to sleep, I reckon you'd call them bunks.
They were kind of cramped and small, but they had those kind of places.
They had places to dance, and they sold liquor…There was a coal oil lamp
in our cabin…They had a place to eat too. It had several decks to it. You
could go upstairs…It had freight, too. It carried freight down in the bottom,
bales of cotton or whatever. When they'd go to Mobile, they usually brought
back a lot of oysters. They brought them back in croker sacks.[16]

Though the railroads had hurt river traffic, they had not dealt a deathblow.
The railroads had brought about a redirection of river traffic, not an end
to it. River landings that had formerly shipped cotton to Mobile now often
shipped it to railheads along the river. Often, in order to increase rail
shipments, the railroads even owned riverboats that ran only from landings
to their railhead. Steamboats still traveled the Upper Tombigbee, but they
were a far cry from the "floating palaces" of the 1850s.

CHAPTER 9

VIENNA AND THE TURN OF THE CENTURY

B y the 1870s, the effect of the railroads on river trade was very apparent at towns that had railroad connections such as Columbus and Aberdeen. Smaller towns and landings away from any railroad continued to rely on the Tombigbee as their main transportation artery. A good example of such a place was Vienna, Alabama, a small community and river landing forty-four miles south of Columbus. By the early 1840s, Henry Connerly was supervisor at a warehouse at Vienna. William Battle Peebles opened a mercantile business in 1844. After his death in 1884, his sons E.B. and W.B. Peebles continued his business interest. In addition, E.B. Peebles operated a river landing at Vienna and was part owner of the steamboat *Vienna* that was built there in 1898 for the Demopolis Vienna Columbus trade.[1]

The dramatic increase in agricultural production and increase in population that occurred during the mid-nineteenth century resulted in a profusion of small settlements and communities about every ten or twelve miles along the Tombigbee. Vienna, Alabama, which was founded during the late 1820s and incorporated in 1841, was one of the communities. In 1875, it was described as "a flourishing little village with two stores."[2] Vienna was located on the east side of the Tombigbee just above the mouth of the Sipsey River. Farmers and planters along the Sipsey would ship their cotton to the Vienna landing on flatboats. Farmers south of the Sipsey could transport their cotton by wagon crossing the Sipsey on a ferry near Vienna. At Vienna, the cotton would be loaded on steamboats to be carried to the Mobile market.

The steamer *Vienna* at Columbus, Mississippi, circa 1902.

As railroads continued to expand during the late 1800s, Vienna found itself bypassed by the railroads. By 1890, the community found that it was forty-four miles south of the Mobile and Ohio and the Georgia Southern Railroads at Columbus, Mississippi, and twenty-five miles north of the Alabama and Great Southern Railroad at Miller's Landing, near Eppes, Alabama.[3] Vienna's trade area was shrinking, but there was still a need to transport local cotton to market. Packet boats continued to call, though in declining size and numbers. The steamboats also began to change their market destinations. Where cotton had once been shipped, mostly to the Mobile market, it was being shipped not only to Mobile but also to railroad connections at Columbus, Eppes/Jones Bluff and Demopolis.[4]

Vienna landing records from 1898 to 1902 document the changes in market destination that was occurring at the small river landings. The first change that is apparent is that although there is little difference in the number of steamboats at Vienna between 1898 and 1899, there is a significant change in destinations. In 1898, most cotton was shipped to the Mobile market, but in 1899 much of the cotton was going not to Mobile but rather to the railroads at Columbus, Eppes and Demopolis. In reviewing only those records showing shipments of twenty-five bales of cotton or more by steamboat from Vienna, this change is very apparent.

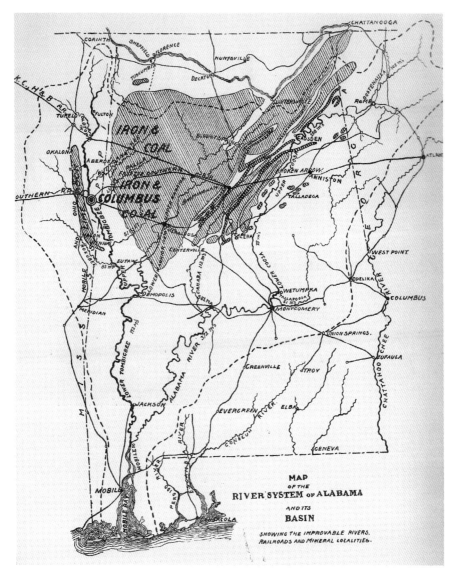

A map of the Mobile River Basin in 1901, showing natural resources, roads and railroads.

Bills of lading from the Vienna Landing Ledger give the names of the steamers, their destinations and freight that was shipped. An examination of shipments of twenty-five or more bales of cotton shows some interesting changes. As fall shipping records were incomplete, the records of only the

A bill of lading for cotton shipped from Vienna Landing, Alabama, to Mobile on the steamer *Frank S. Stone* in 1901.

January shipping season were used for comparative purposes. In January–May 1898, five different boats landed a total of twenty-six times at Vienna. Twenty shipments of cotton were above twenty-five bales, with twelve to Mobile, six to Columbus and one to Demopolis. During the January–May 1899 period, six different boats landed a total of fifty times. Of these steamboats, thirty-one carried twenty-five-plus bales of cotton. Eleven went to Mobile and twenty to Columbus. In January–March 1900, four boats stopped twenty-one times. Of the twenty-five-plus bale shipments, three went to Mobile, ten to Columbus and two to Demopolis. In the January–May 1901 season, a total of three boats made a total of thirty-one stops. Of the twenty-five-plus bale shipments, one went to Mobile, three to Columbus, two to Demopolis and eight to Eppes. In 1902, from January to March 4, boats made a total of sixteen stops, with twenty-five-bale plus destinations being three for Mobile, four for Columbus and one for Demopolis.[5] These figures provide evidence of both a decline in river trade and a change in destination.

The Vienna Landing bills of lading show that cotton was not the only thing being transported by steamboat. The Vienna records show a wide variety of other goods being shipped by steamboat. In January and February 1898, the cargo carried by the *Frank S. Stone* to Vienna from Mobile included cotton, four wheels, an axel, stationery, meat, oil, drugs and oysters. On December 22, 1898, the steamboat *Baltimore* left Vienna for Jones Bluff carrying two kegs of molasses, one trunk, two barrels, two cans of lard and one box of eggs. On at least two occasions, the steamer *City of Columbus* transported packages of money from Vienna to the First State Bank in Columbus. Other items that appear in the Vienna bills of lading were glassware, crockery, a barrel of hides, sacks of corn, coffee, potatoes, barrels of meat, flour, boxes of shoes, whiskey, salt and a case of six-ounce snuff jars. The steamer *Vienna* even once carried a coup of turkeys and a box with a pig in it. Cotton bales and cottonseed, though, remained the principal goods shipped from Vienna.[6] In a 1916 report, the Army Corps of Engineers described Vienna as "Bluff on east bank. No warehouse; no charges, ordinary commerce in cotton and seed."[7]

Thirty years after the full effect of railroad competition was felt in river towns having rail connections, railroads were beginning to have a major

The steamer *Vienna* at the Columbus railroad trestle in 1902 or 1903.

impact on small landings away from the main lines. That impact, though, did not cause the end of river traffic but rather only redirected river traffic from Mobile to railheads. The actual deathblow to steamboats was probably two-pronged. There was construction of branch line railroads that cut small landings off from their trade areas and improvements in rural road construction. Roads that once had been almost impassable during the winter were being improved in an effort to make them all-weather. Small rural landings such as Vienna were no longer solely dependent on river traffic for commerce.

CHAPTER 10
END OF AN ERA

Few steamboats after 1900 were in the Mobile–Upper Tombigbee trade. The expansion of railroads had reduced but not eliminated the need for steamboats. Most of the trade was not directly to and from Mobile but rather between river landings and railroad crossings. However, steamboat trade on the Upper Tombigbee continued to be constrained by the need for high water. For example, on May 8, 1906, the Alabama Cotton Oil Company needed six hundred sacks of cottonseed shipped from Warsaw to Demopolis. There was a rise in the river, and the steamer *City of Mobile* was making a trip to Pickensville and was to charge fifteen dollars per ton to deliver the seed.[1] Among the last boats on the Upper Tombigbee were the *Hard Cash*, *New Haven*, *City of Mobile*, *Mary S. Blees*, *Liberty*, *Hattie B. Moore*, *City of Columbus*, *Ouachita*, *Electra*, *Vienna*, *American*, *John Quill* and *Charles May*.

It is three steamboats—the *Vienna*, the *American* and the *John Quill*—that best exemplify the end of the steam era on the Tombigbee. The *Vienna* was a 176-ton, 155-feet by 276-feet by 4.5-feet stern-wheeler built at Columbus by William Pentecost in 1898. Captain Samuel A. Cosper designed it and supervised construction. He remained its captain after construction.[2] It was built specifically for the Columbus and Demopolis river trade for a stock company principally owned by Joseph Donoghue, W.B. Peebles and W.B. Hopkins. Bert Neville wrote in 1958 that captain Sam Cosper designed and built the *Vienna*.

On January 19, 1906, while headed upriver to Columbus, the *Vienna* struck a snag, called a "dead head," and sank at Moore's Bluff. Although no lives

A view of the Tombigbee bridge and waterfront at Columbus, circa 1905.

The steamer *Vienna* at the Columbus Landing in 1902 or 1903.

The steamer *American* loading cotton at the Columbus Landing in 1907 or 1908.

were lost, it sank with 250 bales of cotton and 2,200 sacks of cottonseed. Attempts to salvage it were unsuccessful because of high water, but most of the cotton and half of the cottonseed was saved.[3] Shortly after its sinking, it was reported that it had struck a snag left from extensive repairs being made upstream to the Columbus railroad bridge.

After the *Vienna* sank, J.E. Stewart of Pickensville bought the steamer *American* and brought it to the Tombigbee. The *American* had been built in Decatur, Alabama, in 1902 and was 158 feet by 27.5 feet by 4.5 feet. It had been constructed for trade on the Tennessee River in the Decatur area.[4]

Beginning in early 1907, the *American* ran on the Upper Tombigbee between Columbus and Demopolis. Low water ended the Columbus trade season in May 1907, and the *American* was leased to H.M. Lindsay. Lindsay put the American in the Alabama River trade about May 21, 1907. The steamboat ran from Mobile to Guilett's Bluff on the Alabama. On January 1, 1908, the *American* returned to the Upper Tombigbee and the Columbus trade. The season ended with low water about March 1, 1908. At that time, Captain Lindsay purchased the boat and moved it back to the Alabama River trade.

The early 1900s saw two large steamer companies try to control the Alabama River trade. They were Quill, Jones and Company and, later,

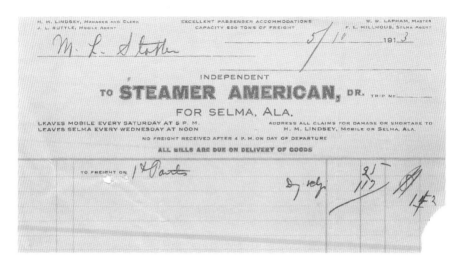

Waybill from the steamer *American* in the Alabama River trade in 1913.

The steamer *New Haven* was in the Columbus-Mobile trade in 1909.

the Birmingham and Gulf Railway Navigation Company. The *American* competed against their Alabama River steamboats as an independent boat.[5] It remained in the Alabama River trade and in 1913 left Mobile every Saturday for Selma. It then would return to Mobile, arriving back on Wednesdays. In 1915, the *American* caught fire and burned at the Mobile wharf.

Following the departure of the *American* from the Upper Tombigbee in May 1908, J.E. Stewart in December 1908 placed the *New Haven*, a smaller steamboat, in the Columbus-Mobile trade. It made regular trips between Columbus and Mobile during the 1908–9 season.[6] The *New Haven*, a small, ninety-two-ton stern-wheeler; the *City of Columbus*, a small, fifty-nine-ton locally owned side-wheeler; and the *Hard Cash*, a large stern-wheeler, were in the Columbus in trade in 1909. The *Hard Cash* had been constructed in 1876 and was owned by the Birmingham and Gulf Railway and Navigation Company. It had been in the Columbus-Mobile trade during the 1890s. By 1900, it was one of the largest steamers operating on the Tombigbee. It was back in the Columbus-Mobile trade in 1907, but in 1908 it was only on the lower part of the river. During the winter season of 1909, it returned to the Upper Tombigbee and made ten trips between Columbus and Mobile.[7]

Passenger traffic was much less important to steamboats than it had been, and that was reflected by a slower but safer speed for the boats. In December 1908, the steamer *New Haven* took ten days to travel from Mobile to Columbus. Unlike the steamers of the boom years, the *New Haven* tied

The steamer *John Quill* on the Tombigbee above Demopolis in 1922.

up at night. The bulk of its cargo was 150 bales of cotton and 1,500 sacks of cottonseed.[8] On Thursday, February 18, 1909, the steamer *Hard Cash* arrived in Columbus, having left Mobile on the previous Sunday. It departed Columbus on Friday with a cargo consisting of 150 tons of fertilizer, 50 bales of linters and twenty tons of horse feed.

One of the last packet boats in the Columbus trade was the *John Quill*. Built in 1907 in Jefferson, Indiana, it was a 270-ton stern-wheeler. It was 168 feet by 35 feet by 4.9 feet in dimension. In 1908, the Birmingham and Gulf Railway and Navigation Company bought the steamer. It became the "Bigbee River packet, making two trips a week, leaving Mobile every Tuesday and Saturday nights for Demopolis, in opposition to the Staples Line's *Mary S. Blees*." At that time, the *American* was the Columbus–Demopolis boat, the *City of Mobile* was the Mobile Tuesday packet to Selma and Montgomery and the *W.J. Bertha* was the Saturday packet for Selma.[9] In 1912, the *John Quill* was in the Upper Tombigbee trade and arrived in Columbus from Mobile.

The steamer *James T. Staples* at the Mobile Wharf, circa 1910.

The *John Quill* was still in the Lower Tombigbee trade in 1913. On January 9, 1913, the steamer *James T. Staples* blew up near Powe's Landing on the Lower Tombigbee. Twenty-six people were killed and twenty-one were injured. The *John Quill* arrived soon after, rescued the survivors and carried them to Mobile.[10] That was the last major steamboat disaster on the Tombigbee.

The *John Quill* remained in the Mobile Tombigbee trade to Demopolis and, at times, to Tuscaloosa. On June 12, 1916, it struck a rock in the Warrior River and sank. It was raised and returned to river trade. The *John Quill* was finally lost when it sank at Twelve Mile Island in the Mobile River in 1929.[11] Thus was the end of one of the last packet boats in the Upper Tombigbee trade.

In February 1913, the steam-powered stern-wheel towboat *James L. Hale* arrived in Columbus and continued on to Aberdeen before returning to Demopolis. It arrived with a cargo of cotton and cottonseed. It returned to Demopolis carrying ninety tons of fertilizer. The Demopolis Lumber Company owned the *Hale*, and it was eventually converted to diesel power. It was still operating on the Lower Tombigbee out of Demopolis in 1955.[12]

The *Charles May* was probably the last commercial trade steamboat at Columbus. The *May* arrived in 1914 and advertised that it would run regularly between Columbus and Mobile. Records do not name any packet boats in the Columbus trade after 1914.[13] However, Army Corps of Engineers reports reflect that as late as 1918 there was a small quantity of cotton and cottonseed shipped from the Upper Tombigbee. By 1919, except for lumber, commercial river traffic had ended at Columbus and above, but some steamboat traffic continued below Columbus into the 1920s. Small steamers involved in the lumber trade on the Upper Tombigbee continued to operate but were the only remaining commercial steamboats on that part of the river.

Annual Reports of the Chief of Engineers to Congress detail the decrease in river commerce on the Tombigbee above Demopolis. In 1892, 3,000 tons of cotton, 2,916 tons of grain and 7,928 tons of general merchandise were shipped by steamer from the Upper Tombigbee. The total tonnage of all shipments above Demopolis was 19,009 tons. The decrease in river traffic was apparent in a 1909 Army Corps of Engineers report discussing commerce in cotton, cottonseed timber, farm supplies and general merchandise on the Tombigbee:

During 1906, 414,932 tons of these commodities were handled on the river between Demopolis and the mouth of the river, 9,775 tons between Columbus, Miss., and Demopolis, and 1,000 tons above Columbus, the latter consisting of heading bolts and general merchandise.

By 1918, only 417 tons of commodities and general merchandise were shipped from above Demopolis. The organization reported that Pickensville was considered as the usual "upper limit of navigation for boats of any considerable size." Timber had become the main upper river commerce. Rafting of logs continued, and in 1918 16,960 tons of logs and 10,000 tons of stave bolts were shipped from the Upper Tombigbee.[14] Steamer traffic from Demopolis on down continued through the 1920s until it was totally replaced by diesel propeller-driven towboats.

Above Demopolis, the uncertainties of the river trade could not stand up to all-weather roads and newly popular motor vehicles. The imminent death of steamboat traffic was apparent by 1912, which happened to be the time of the start of construction of the "macadam" all-weather roads in the region.

The steamer *Corinne* at the Columbus landing in 1905. It was an Aberdeen boat in the lumber trade on the Upper Tombigbee between 1905 and 1909.

A towboat near Demopolis in 1921.

The Army Corps of Engineers reported that during 1914

> [t]*he Tombigbee River, from Demopolis, Ala., to Aberdeen, Miss., is open to steamboat navigation during six months of the year. At present small boats with barges navigate the river in the vicinity of Columbus, for about nine months of the year, and the regular packet steamers from Mobile navigate the river below Columbus for about six months of the year. A light-draft steamer made regular trips from Columbus, operating above and below it, through the winter season.*[15]

That light draft steamer was probably the ninety-four-ton stern-wheeler *Charles May*, which ran from Columbus to Mobile in 1914. It is the last packet boat to leave a record of scheduled trips to Columbus. In 1913, the Army Corps of Engineers described the landings in use on the Tombigbee River from Demopolis, Alabama, to Columbus, Mississippi[16]:

TABLE 2. IMPORTANT RIVER LANDINGS BETWEEN DEMOPOLIS AND COLUMBUS.

Landing Name	River Mile	Description	Distance to Nearest Railroad	Highway Conditions to Landing
Demopolis	230	high bluff; town warehouses, cotton compresses, large commerce; station on Southern Ry; no improved water terminal or wharves; no charge for landing	Southern RR at terminal	poor road to water terminal
Miller's	273.6	bluff on east bank; warehouse compress and oil mill at Eppes; Alabama Great Southern RR; no charge for landing	Alabama Great Southern RR station	poor road to landing
Gainesville	290.8	bluff on west bank; town; has warehouse; no charge for landing	Alabama, Tennessee & Northern RR, 7 miles	poor road to landing
Warsaw	303	bluff on west bank; warehouse; charges ten cents per cotton bale at landing	Alabama, Tennessee & Northern RR, 3 miles	poor road to landing
Vienna	314.4	bluff on east bank; no warehouse; no charge for landing	Alabama, Tennessee & Northern RR, 3 miles	sandy road
Stone's Ferry	328.7	bluff on west bank; warehouse; charges ten cents per cotton bale at landing; Alabama, Tennessee & Northern RR crossing	Alabama, Tennessee & Northern RR terminal	sandy road

Landing Name	River Mile	Description	Distance to Nearest Railroad	Highway Conditions to Landing
Memphis	336.8	bluff on west bank; no warehouse; no charge for landing	Alabama, Tennessee & Northern RR, 7 miles	prairie road
Pickensville	348.2	bluff on west bank; warehouse; charges ten cents per cotton bale at landing	Alabama, Tennessee & Northern RR, 8 miles	sandy road
Columbus	379	bluff on east bank; town warehouse; three oil mills; cotton compress; large commerce; no improved water terminal or wharves; no charge for landing	Mobile & Ohio and Southern RR terminals	poor road to water terminal

A view of cotton being hauled by wagon over an unimproved road in Alabama prior to 1910.

An unimproved Lowndes County, Mississippi road in 1912.

While the railroads had first ended the golden age of Tombigbee steamboats, all-weather roads and more reliable motor vehicles finished off river trade. Transportation at the turn of the century in rural areas lacking rail service was little different than during the early 1800s. Goods were still carried by wagon over roads that became almost impassable in bad weather.

In 1911, the *New York Times* reported that "[t]he year 1910 will go down in history as the one in which the freight vehicle, particularly of the gasoline type, first came into generally accepted notice."[17]

By 1912, all-weather roads were being constructed across the Upper Tombigbee Valley, and by 1914, the day of the steamboat had all but ended. The Tombigbee River and the railroad were no longer the only way to get to market.

It was not until the construction of the Tennessee Tombigbee Waterway that commercial traffic returned to the Upper Tombigbee River at Columbus and Aberdeen. Not long after the waterway opened in 1985, a stern-wheel vessel, the *Delta Queen*, returned to the Upper Tombigbee.

TRIP STATEMENT OF THE
STEAMER *LIBERTY*

T his appendix is an accounting of the receipts and expenditures of the
164-foot-long stern-wheel steamboat *Liberty* and a barge on a trip from
Mobile to Demopolis, followed by a return trip to Mobile, from March 30
to April 3, 1907.

Receipts were $218.75 for passengers and $1,216.00 for freight, totaling
$1,434.75. Expenses included $139.25 for stores (coffee, fish, bread, milk,
pork, eggs and produce), $145.50 for fuel, $448.75 for coal from Mobile
and the balance for wood from river landings and $511.85 for wages. Total
expenses were $1,020.05, leaving a net profit of $414.70. It is interesting
that the expenses included no amount for depreciation, repair or insurance.

WAGES OF THE OFFICERS AND CREW ON A ROUND TRIP OF THE STEAMER *LIBERTY*
(IN DOLLARS).
FROM MOBILE TO DEMOPOLIS, ALABAMA, IN 1907.

Officers

Captain	26.25
Clerk	26.25
Clerk	17.50
Clerk	17.50

APPENDIX 1

Statement of Receipts and Expenditures

OF STEAMER *Liberty & Barge*

M. Jackson Master. *B. J. Fisher* Clerk.

Trip No. *17* From *Maple* to *Reneedale* and return

From the *30* day of *March* 190*7* to the *3* day of *April* 190*7* inclusive.

RECEIPTS

FREIGHT—"Up,"	1134 20		
" "Down,	81 80	1216 00	
PASSAGE—"Up,"	130 75		
" "Down,"	88 00	218 75	1434 75
Cash Letters			

EXPENDITURES

Stores,	139 25			
Feed,	145 50			
Expense,	223 45	508 20		
Wages: Officers,	237 85			
Cabin Crew,	48 50			
Deck Crew,	204 50			
Firemen,	21 00	511 85	1020 05	
Labor,				

Net Profits. ✓ 414 70

E. & O. E.

Trip Statement from the steamer *Liberty* in 1907.

Pilot	26.25
Pilot	26.25
Engineer	23.35
Engineer	23.35
2 boys, Strikers	8.00
Mate	21.00
Carpenter	17.50
Watchman	9.35
Total	**237.85**

Cabin Crew

Steward	8.00
Cook	20.00

The steamer *Liberty* on the Alabama River at Selma in 1910 or 1911.

Pantry	4.00
C Maid	4.00
5 Cabin Boys	12.50
Total	**48.50**

Deck Crew

4 men, Stevedores	42.00
20 men	160.00
1 boy, Decker	2.50
Total	**204.50**

Firemen

2 men, Firemen	21.00

Final Total	**511.85**

APPENDIX 2
THE 1877–1881 HARGROVE
SHIPPING RECORDS

The records of the W.H. Hargrove estate in the Lowndes County, Mississippi Chancery Court Records at the Billups-Garth Archives of the Columbus-Lowndes Public Library document the shipment of cotton by both rail and water from 1877 to 1881. The cotton was from Lowndes County, Mississippi, and was being sold through Baker, Lawler & Company cotton factors of Mobile, Alabama. Cotton was being shipped to Mobile and probably to railheads at Eppes and Demopolis, Alabama. Though the cotton factor was in Mobile, one of the steamboats being used was the *William S. Holt*, a boat partially owned by the Central Railroad and Banking Company of Georgia. Its rail line linked with the Tombigbee River near Demopolis. Also an aid in determining destination is the knowledge that a three-day turnaround by some steamboats was too short a time frame for a trip from Columbus to Mobile but was about right for railheads at Eppes and Demopolis. The names of the steamboats are given as provided in the estate records. The complete names of the steamboats are the *William S. Holt, Lotus No. 2, John T. Moore, Brandish Johnson, Lulu D., Lillie Lou, Era, Ruth* and *W.H. Gardner.*

APPENDIX 2

THE SHIPMENTS OF HARGROVE ESTATE COTTON FROM
LOWNDES COUNTY, MISSISSIPPI

Date   Shipped by Steamboat or Railroad

1877–1878 Season

1877

October 8	Mobile and Ohio Railroad
November 3	Mobile and Ohio Railroad
7	Mobile and Ohio Railroad
8	Mobile and Ohio Railroad
10	St. *Holt*
29	St. *Lotus No. 2*
December 3	St. *Holt*
12	St. *Holt*

1878

January 18	St. *Moore*
21	St. *Holt*
24	St. *Lotus No. 2*
28	St. *Holt*
February 5	St. *Holt*
12	St. *Holt*
15	St. *Holt*
19	St. *Holt*
23	St. *Johnson*
April 9	St. *Holt*
May 14	St. *Holt*

1878–1879 Season

1878

December 6	St. *Lulu D.*
8	St. *Fleta*
23	St. *Johnson*

1879

January 23	St. *Moore*
23	St. *Lulu D.*
27	St. *Lulu D.*

1879–1880 Season

1879

October 2	Mobile and Ohio Railroad
11	Mobile and Ohio Railroad
November 21	St. *Ruth*
29	St. *Lillie Lou*
December 3	St. *Lillie Lou*
8	St. *Lulu D.*
12	St. *Lillie Lou*
18	St. *Lulu D.*

1880

January 3	St. *Lotus No. 2*
17	St. *Era*
19	St. *Ruth*
February 14	St. *Era*
March 20	St. *Hale*

APPENDIX 2

1880–1881 Season

<u>1880</u>

December 6	St. *Era*
9	St. *Johnson*
14	St. *Ruth*
23	St. *Lotus No. 2*

<u>1881</u>

January 20	St. *Gardner*
February 12	St. *Gardner*

APPENDIX 3
TOMBIGBEE DRAWBRIDGES

The first bridge over the Tombigbee at Columbus, Mississippi, was not a drawbridge but rather a wooden covered bridge that came off the top of the high river bluff. The bridge was built in 1842 by Horace King, an African American engineer. The piers of the bridge in the river channel were sixty-five feet high. However, at high water the bridge became a hazard to navigation. The remedy to the obstruction of the river navigation was the building of drawbridges.

The drawbridge on the Alabama River at Selma, opened for a steamer to pass upriver in 1905.

As the Tombigbee was a river open to navigation, it became necessary to obtain approval from the War Department (Army Corps of Engineers) for bridge construction. In 1888, the Georgia Pacific Railway Company submitted plans for the construction of a railroad bridge near Columbus. Correspondence contained in the secretary of war's *Messages and Documents Submitted to Congress at the Fiftieth Congress,* vol. II, part 4, detail what was required. "The plan submitted covers the whole of the waterway of the river with its draw-spans, which, as nearly as can be ascertained from the drawings, are of sufficient width for the purposes of navigation at the proposed new location." The requirement for bridges on the Upper Tombigbee to be drawbridges continued into the late 1920s; a 1928 highway bridge over the Tombigbee constructed at Columbus is a drawbridge.

A DIRECTORY OF STEAMBOATS ON THE UPPER TOMBIGBEE

The Upper Tombigbee, Little Tombigbee and Upper Tombigbee refer to that part of the Tombigbee River above Demopolis, Alabama. Steamboat traffic above Demopolis began in 1822 and ended about 1920.

Aberdeen, a stern-wheel freight boat built in 1909; operated on the Upper Tombigbee 1910–11; sold to the Alabama River.

Aberdeen, 209-ton side-wheeler built in 1848; 1,300-bale capacity; snagged Devils Shoals, Alabama River, 12/21/1851, no deaths; Aberdeen trade in fall of 1849; made thirteen trips to Columbus, December 1850–May 1851.

Admiral, 242-ton side-wheeler built in 1843; collided at Clarkville, Arkansas, 12/28/1847.

Admiral, 275-ton side-wheeler built in 1859; 1,412-bale capacity; formerly *William S. Barry*, captured by the United States in 1864; renamed *Admiral* 7/5/1865; abandoned 1872.

Agnes, 85-ton side-wheeler built in 1840; 1,000-bale capacity; abandoned 1846.

Alabama, built circa 1855; 1,871-bale capacity; during the 1855–56 season, it made two trips to Aberdeen; this steamer is not listed in Lloyd's directory of Mobile steamboats compiled in 1855; on the Mississippi River there is a listing for a 298-ton steamboat built in 1851 named *Alabama*.

Alabama, 162-ton side-wheeler built in 1841; 910-bale capacity; was in the Columbus trade in 1845 and the Aberdeen trade during late 1840s; lost in 1847.

Typical Tombigbee River steamboat loaded with cotton, circa 1905.

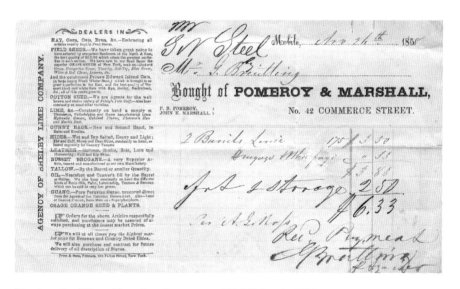

Two barrels of lime shipped on the steamer *Alfred G. Ross* in 1858.

Alamo, 66-ton side-wheeler built in 1850; lost at Mobile, Alabama, 6/1/1856.

Albatross, side-wheeler built in 1844; 1,513-bale capacity; in Columbus trade (three trips) 1850–51.

Alfred G. Ross, 126-ton stern-wheeler built in 1858; it was in the Aberdeen trade spring of 1859; snagged, Demopolis, Alabama, 9/27/1860 but raised.

Alice, stern-wheeler built circa 1876; 500-bale capacity; built in Columbus for the Columbus trade.

Alice M., 185-ton side-wheeler built in 1865; 479-bale capacity or higher; it was in the Columbus trade during the 1865–66 seasons; stranded Galveston, Texas, 10/3/1867.

Alice Vivian, 376-ton side-wheeler built in 1856; 2,400-bale capacity or higher; considered the fastest steamer on the Little Bigby; it was in the Mobile–Warrior River packet during the late 1850s; during the 1862–63 season it made two trips to Columbus before being converted to a blockade-runner; in January 1863 it carried Confederate ordnance from Columbus to Mobile; it made one trip to Havana, Cuba, before being captured by the USS *De Soto* in August 1863; it was carrying the staff of General James E. Slaughter, CSA, when captured; was probably the steamboat *Alice Vivian* that was transporting supplies and ran aground on a sandbar on the Red River on 4/12/1864; in February 1865 it helped transport the Seventy-sixth Illinois Regiment from Lake Pontchartrain to Fort Morgan to Fort Barrancas near Pensacola; after the war ended, it was sold and redocumented as the *South* on 2/3/1866; it was abandoned 1867.

Allegheny, 45-ton side-wheeler built in 1823; snagged and sank, twelve miles below Columbus, Mississippi, 5/16/1825 on its way from Hamilton to Mobile; no lives lost.

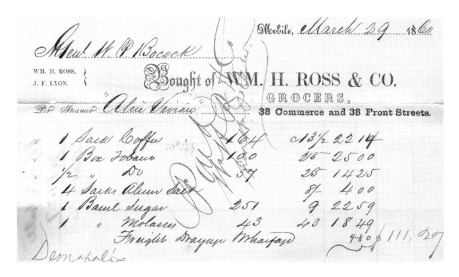

Goods shipped on the *Alice Vivian* from Mobile to Demopolis in 1860.

An 1846 advertisement from the *Mobile Register* for the steamer *Amaranth*.

Alpha, a barge.

Amaranth, 185-ton side-wheeler built in 1845; 1,400-bale capacity; snagged 7/14/1848.

Amazon, side-wheeler built circa 1847; 1,200-bale capacity; in Columbus trade 1850–51; sold circa 1852.

American, 152-ton side-wheeler built in 1827; abandoned 1836.

American, stern-wheeler built in 1902; its hull was 158 feet by 27.5 feet by 4.5 feet; it first operated between Decatur, Alabama, and St. Louis; in 1903 it became a Vicksburg–Yazoo City packet; it came to the Upper Tombigbee trade in early 1907 to replace the steamer *Vienna*, which had struck a snag and sunk below Columbus; in May 1907, when the river stage at Columbus became low, it was transferred downriver to H.M. Lindsay and placed in the Alabama River trade; it was then returned to Columbus and the Upper Tombigbee about 1/1/1908; it mostly ran between Columbus and Demopolis until 3/1/1908, when it was sold to Lindsay and the Alabama River trade; it burned at Mobile, Alabama, 4/4/1915.

Andrew Jackson, 98-ton side-wheeler built in 1833; 450-bale capacity; snagged Mobile, Alabama, 5/16/1838; it was the Regular Cotton Gin Port–Mobile packet in 1836 and in the Columbus trade in 1837.

A Directory of Steamboats on the Upper Tombigbee

The steamer *American* at the Tombigbee Landing at Gainesville, Alabama, in 1907 or 1908.

Anna Calhoun, 133-ton side-wheeler built in 1835; 865-bale capacity; Upper Tombigbee trade in 1838 and 1840; in 1843, it was the weekly Vienna-Fairfield-Memphis-Pickensville packet; it would leave Mobile Wednesday evening and arrive at Pickensville on Friday evening; abandoned 1845.

Ariel, 169-ton side-wheeler built in 1854; 1,000-bale capacity; was in the Aberdeen trade during the 1855–56 season, when it made eleven trips, and also during November–December season of 1859; its cook, Sam Crote, and bartender, George Lawdermilk, were among the most noted on the river; it passed to Confederate control in 1861.

Ark, 122-ton side-wheeler built in 1845; abandoned 1850.

Ark, flatboat on Little Tombigbee, February 1859; 356-bale capacity.

Arkansas, built in about 1840; 1,042-bale capacity; renovated in Mobile, 1842; Aberdeen trade during mid- to late 1840s.

Arkansas, 51-ton stern-wheeler built in 1820; 600-bale capacity; it would normally carry 400 to 600 barrels of merchandise; Columbus trade in 1824; snagged near Mobile in 1827.

Arkansas No. 5, 162-ton side-wheeler built in 1845; snagged 6/5/1856.

Atlanta, 330-ton side-wheeler; snagged Belfast Chute, Tombigbee River, 1/12/1877; in Upper Tombigbee trade 1874 as regular Tuesday packet to Pickensville.

Avalanche, 143-ton side-wheeler built in 1837; it was in the Columbus trade 1841–42; scrapped 1843.

Azile, 132-ton stern-wheeler built in 1852, 900-bale capacity or higher; during 1855–56 season, made nine trips to Aberdeen; it struck a large log, which pierced its hull at Ten Mile Shoals and sank 3/7/1856; two people

Left: Account for forty bales of cotton shipped to Mobile in 1838 aboard the steamer *Anna Calhoun*.

Below: A waybill for goods shipped to Aberdeen, Mississippi, on the steamer *Ariel* in 1858.

killed; there is a lawsuit about this steamer's salvage after it sank filed in Lowndes County, Mississippi Circuit Court case no. 10422.

Balize, 103-ton side-wheeler built in 1823; a schooner converted to steam power in 1824; it escorted steamer *Henderson* when the *Henderson* carried La Fayette down the Alabama River in April 1824; *Balize* collided with the *Henderson* on 4/27/1825, above Claiborne on the Alabama River.

Baltimore, stern-wheeler built in 1887 for the Gulf Coast oyster trade; it was 104 feet by 19 feet by 4.7 feet; it was bought by the Black Warrior Lumber Company and was at Demopolis during the late 1890s; it transported cotton from Vienna to Eppes in December 1898 and from Vienna to Demopolis in 1899; in 1908, it was dismantled at Demopolis; its engines were used in the steamer *Charles May* that was built at West Bend, Alabama, in 1913.

Belfast, 156-ton stern-wheeler built in 1857; Columbus and Aberdeen trade 1865–66 and 1866–67 seasons; it was the subject of a noted U.S. Supreme Court case in 1868; it concerned a robbery of cotton being carried on it from Columbus to Mobile in January 1866; it burned at Belfast Chute, Tombigbee River, 3/7/1868.

Belle Gates, 278-ton side-wheeler built in 1851 for Aberdeen trade; ran from Mobile to Columbus in forty hours fifteen minutes; it was in the Aberdeen trade 1852–54 but was sold downriver in 1855; G.W. Lawdermilk served as its bartender; passed to Confederate control, 1861.

Belle of Attakapos, 246-ton side-wheeler built in 1841; 1,200-bale capacity; abandoned 1847.

Belle Poule, 157-ton side-wheeler built in 1841; 1,000-bale capacity; it was controlled by Aberdeen interest; Aberdeen trade 1843–44; snagged near Pickensville, Alabama, March 1846 and sank; another account reflects sinking at Mobile 7/2/1849.

Ben Lee, 122-ton stern-wheeler built in 1852; 700-bale capacity; during 1855–56 season it made nine trips to Aberdeen; snagged at Mobile, Alabama, 12/13/1856.

Billy Collins, 60-ton stern-wheeler built in 1872; ran from Columbus to Miller's Landing (Eppes) to connect to Alabama Great Southern Railroad during the 1879–82 seasons.

Black Diamond, built about 1860; Columbus trade 1865–66; it surrendered to Union forces on the Tombigbee River on 5/9/1865; burned 3/3/1866; entire cargo lost.

Black Hawk, 800-bale capacity.

Bloomer, 70-ton built in 1852; 600-bale capacity; it made two trips to Aberdeen during the 1855–56 season and was in Aberdeen trade during 1857–58 season.

Boliver, 58-ton side-wheeler built in 1827, 600-barrel capacity; it was in the Tombigbee trade in 1828; abandoned 1832.

Bourbon, 171-ton side-wheeler built in 1843; 900-balc capacity or higher; abandoned 1851.

Brandish Johnson, 412-ton side-wheeler built in 1869 for the New Orleans–Red River trade; 1,600-bale capacity; in 1876, it was purchased and moved to Mobile; it was at Pickensville in January 1877 and was in the Columbus trade 1878 and 1880; at that time, the Columbus landing it used was Turner's Cut; it burned at Jackson, Alabama, August 1887.

Bristol, 149-ton side-wheeler built in 1841; 700-bale capacity or higher; it was in the Aberdeen trade in 1843; abandoned 1849.

Cahawba, 145-ton side-wheeler built in 1837; 900-bale capacity; Columbus trade in 1839.

Callie C., small stern-wheeler operating in lumber business at Aberdeen 1906.

Canebrake, 162-ton side-wheeler built in 1840; stranded Warsaw, Alabama, Tombigbee River, 1/1/1845.

Captain Sumpter, on the Tombigbee in 1836.

Carolina, 177-ton built in 1836; 1,600-bale capacity; Pickensville trade 1844; abandoned 1844.

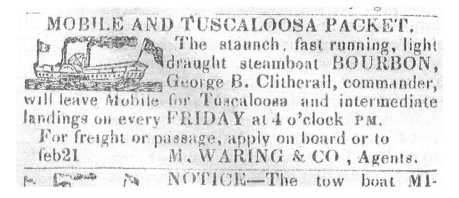

An 1846 advertisement from the *Mobile Register* for the steamer *Bourbon*.

A letter stamped "PACKET CANEBRAKE" showing that it was carried by that steamboat.

Carolina, 187-ton side-wheeler built in 1832; abandoned 1840.

Carrier, 140-ton stern-wheeler built in 1883; Pickensville trade March 1894.

Caspian, 199-ton side-wheeler built in 1832; 900-bale capacity; snagged Mobile, Alabama, 5/6/1840.

Catawba, 112-ton side-wheeler built in 1827; abandoned 1831.

Champion, 158-ton side-wheeler built in 1853; 1,800-bale capacity or higher; Columbus-Mobile packet 1853; during 1855–56 season it made nine trips to Aberdeen; after the burning of the *Eliza Battle*, it brought the remains of six or seven of the lost back upriver; it was abandoned late 1858.

Charles L. Bass, 103-ton side-wheeler built in 1836; 477-bale capacity or higher; snagged at Mobile, Alabama, 11/22/1842.

Charles May, 94-ton stern-wheeler built in 1913 by Captain Charles May; it had a 150-horsepower engine taken from the abandoned steamer *Baltimore* and was 134.8 feet by 26.9 feet by 3.5; it was one of the last (if not the very last) stern-wheel packet boats in the Columbus trade; records show it at Columbus in 1914 and sinking at Mobile about 1916.

Cherokee, 337-ton side-wheeler built in 1859; named after Cherokee Jemison of Tuscaloosa; known as a fast boat that liked to race, it was able to make

A dray ticket from the steamer *Cherokee* in 1860.

one trip to Columbus in April 1863; abandoned 1874 on the north bank of the Dog River below Mobile; a steamer named *Cherokee* was reported burned by Union forces at Montgomery.

Chickasaw, 149-ton side-wheeler built in 1834; 1,000-bale capacity or higher; converted to barge 2/5/1842.

Chippewa, 150-ton side-wheeler built in 1832; 605-bale capacity or higher; snagged Cape Girardeau, Missouri, 3/25/1841.

City of Columbus, 59-ton side-wheeler built in Columbus by A.P. Pressley in 1883; in the Columbus-Vienna trade; burned and sank at Columbus wharf in 1911.

City of Demopolis, in the Vienna-Demopolis trade circa 1900.

City of Mobile, 209-ton stern-wheeler built in 1898; in August 1908 it was the Mobile Tuesday packet for Selma and Montgomery; it was destroyed by the 1916 Mobile hurricane.

Clara, 185-ton side-wheeler built in 1848; 1,500-bale capacity or higher; burned at Cincinnati, Ohio, 9/8/1853; Columbus-Mobile packet 1849; Aberdeen trade in fall of 1850; made fifteen trips to Columbus during 1850–51 season.

Clara, 343-ton side-wheeler built in 1864; Columbus and Aberdeen trade in 1869; snagged Missouri River, 5/23/1870.

Clara Dunning, side-wheeler built in 1864.

Clarion, 32-ton built in 1841; abandoned 1846.

Clarion, 217-ton side-wheeler built in 1842; 1,100-bale capacity or higher; burned Guyandotte, Georgia, 5/1/1845.

The steamer *City of Mobile* at the Mobile Wharf in 1908.

A letter carried to Waverly, Mississippi, by the steamboat *Clara*, circa 1850.

Clipper, 242-ton built in 1862; Tuesday packet for Vienna, February 1862; Warsaw and Vienna packet in 1863; burned in the "Cut Off," 10/5/1865 with eight lives lost.

Colonel Fremont, 74-ton stern-wheeler built in 1850; snagged Tombigbee River, 10/24/1854.

Columbus, 134-ton side-wheeler built in 1836; 900-bale capacity or higher; Named for Columbus, Mississippi; it was in the Columbus trade in November 1837; Columbus newspaper described it as "one of the most beautiful boats upon the Southern waters"; it was abandoned in 1842.

Columbus Hornet, keelboat, Columbus-Mobile trade in 1821.

Commerce, 170-ton side-wheeler built in 1834; 800-bale capacity or higher; abandoned 1842.

Coosa Belle, 229-ton stern-wheeler built in 1855; snagged Bridgeport, Alabama River, 4/24/1860.

Cora, stern-wheeler built in 1864; Columbus trade 1865–66.

Corinne, 121-ton side-wheeler built in 1849; 800-bale capacity or higher; abandoned 1856.

Cornelia C., a stern-wheeler, used about 1905–9 in lumber business at Aberdeen; in 1906, deckhand Ed Hillard was washing his clothes on the lower deck when he fell into the Tombigbee and drowned.

Correo, 89-ton side-wheeler built in 1847; 700-bale capacity; snagged Mobile, Alabama, 5/20/1856; four trips Columbus-Mobile trade, 1850–51 season.

Corsair, 119-ton built in 1830; in 1831 was in Columbus-Mobile trade; abandoned 1836.

Cotton Gin Cutter, first recorded keelboat from Cotton Gin Port to Mobile, January 1820; in Mobile–Cotton Gin Port trade, 1821–22.

Cotton Plant, 72-ton side-wheeler built in 1821; first steamer to Columbus, probably 1822 and possibly as late as spring of 1823; first steamer to Cotton Gin Port in April 1824; Tuscaloosa trade under Capt Chandler 1821 and considered the first steamboat to reach there in 1821; sank at Whites Landing, Warrior River, 5/7/1828.

Courier, 142-ton side-wheeler built in 1831; abandoned 1839.

Cremona, 268-ton side-wheeler built in 1852, over 200 feet long; during 1855–56 season it made two trips to Aberdeen; in spring of 1859 was Mobile Tuesday evening packet for Aberdeen and Columbus; during the 1856–57 season it was the first steamer with a calliope to arrive at Aberdeen;

An accounting of cotton carried to Mobile by the steamer *Cremona* in 1854.

passed to Confederate control in 1861 and was used to transport supplies; intentionally sunk by Confederate navy in Mobile Bay in 1864 to block ship channel.

Creole, side-wheeler built in 1839; it was in the Upper Tombigbee trade about 1847.

Crusader, 120-ton side-wheeler built in 1836; exploded near Mobile 6/20/1837, twelve deaths; after the explosion, it anchored and was towed to Mobile by the steamer *Mobile*.

Cuba, 286-ton side-wheeler built in 1850; 1,700-bale capacity; it made sixteen trips to Columbus, 1850–51 season, as the Mobile Saturday packet for Columbus; also Mobile-Columbus trade, Robert Otis, master, December 1852 and September 1852; during the 1852 season it would leave Mobile at 5:00 p.m. on Monday and arrive in Columbus Wednesday evening; in August 1852, it was repaired and repainted; it was noted for racing and

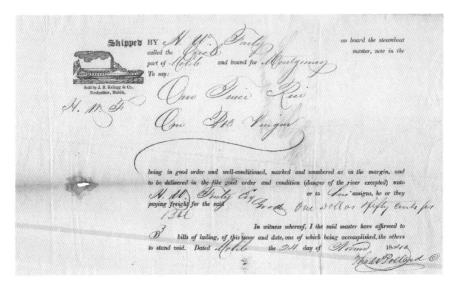

A waybill from the steamer *Creole* in 1840.

it was once said that "it runs like a scared dog"; snagged Davis Landing, Alabama River, 4/20/1856, seven lives lost.

C.W. Anderson, built in on 1876, it was in the Tombigbee trade in 1889; it burned at Mobile in 1892.

C.W. Dorrance, 340-ton side-wheeler built in 1857; 1,300-bale capacity or higher; Columbus and Aberdeen trade 1865–68; it hit the wreck of *Senator No. 2* and sank in the Alabama River in 1870 at Young's Landing.

Czar, 358-ton built in 1855; 194 feet by 33 feet with hold depth of 6.5 feet; 2,200-bale capacity; passed to Confederate control in 1861.

Dallas, 244-ton side-wheeler built in 1842; abandoned 1849.

Dandridge, built in about 1865; 1,000-bale capacity; Columbus trade 1865–66 season.

Desoto, built in about 1868 and was in the Upper Tombigbee trade in 1869.

D.F. Day, built in about 1851; 1,400-bale capacity.

D.F. Tally, 263-ton built in 1870; it was in the Upper Tombigbee trade to Demopolis, Vienna and Columbus 1898–1901.

Dispatch, 105-ton side-wheeler built in 1835; stranded Mobile, Alabama, 12/30/1842.

Dove, a steamer named *Dove* came to Columbus during the 1865–66 season.

Dove, 140-ton built in about 1881; 500-bale capacity; Mobile-Macon in January and February 1883.

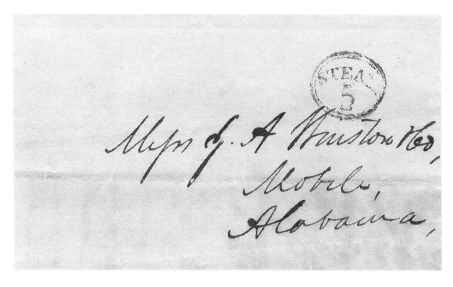

Steamboat postal marking stamped on a letter from Columbus to Mobile. The contents of the letter indicate that it was carried on the steamer *Cuba*.

A December 1845 advertisement from the *Mobile Register* for the steamer *Dallas*.

Duncan, 212-ton built in Columbus, Mississippi, and in Columbus trade 1840–42.

Duquesne or *Du Quesne*, 140-ton built in 1839; 900-bale capacity or higher; abandoned 1850; Mobile-Columbus-Plymouth packet in 1843.

A December 1843 advertisement from the *Columbus Whig* for the steamer *Du Quesne*.

Echo, side-wheeler built in 1837; 900-bale capacity.

Eighth of January, 98-ton side-wheeler built in 1846; 762-bale capacity; regular Cotton Gin Port packet 1847–48; sank, Choctowhatchee River, 1857.

Electra, 372-ton stern-wheeler built in 1897; Columbus trade in 1912; renamed *Sunny South* in 1914 and lost at Mobile in hurricane of 1916.

Eliza, 321-ton side-wheeler built in 1844; 1,500-bale capacity; a fast steamer that could run from Mobile to Demopolis in eighteen to twenty hours; in 1845 it was the Mobile Tuesday packet for Gainesville and advertised "superior accommodations" including "double bedsteads"; it was the Warsaw packet in 1846; abandoned 1852 or '58.

Eliza Battle, 316-ton side-wheeler built in 1852; 2,000-bale capacity or higher; in 1853 it was the Warsaw Mobile packet; it caught fire near Kemp's

A waybill for goods shipped on the steamer *Eliza*.

An 1854 waybill from the steamer *Eliza Battle*.

Landing, Tombigbee River, 3/1/1858, on a freezing night when river was flooded; thirty-three lives and 1,300 bales of cotton lost; fire probably started by sparks from passing steamer *Warrior*; those lost included one person from Columbus and two from Chickasaw County; the steamer *Magnolia* carried the survivors to Mobile.

Eliza No. 2, 349-ton side-wheeler built in 1851; 900-bale capacity or higher; snagged Tennessee, 1/25/1855, but during 1855–56 season it made three trips to Aberdeen; in Camargo trade in 1852.

Elizabeth, keelboat, Cotton Gin Port–Mobile, 1821–22.

Elnora, built prior 1866; 800-bale capacity or higher; Columbus trade, 1865–66 season.

E.M. Bicknell, 203-ton side-wheeler built in 1857; Columbus and Aberdeen trade 1865–67 and in the Columbus trade 1868–69; abandoned 1871.

Emblem, 120-ton side-wheeler built in 1836; 785-bale capacity; foundered Mobile, Alabama, 4/18/1839, five lives lost; Mobile-Columbus trade in 1839.

Emma Lee, owned by E.B. Mason & Company of Columbus, from June 1870 to May 1871; in an 1872 Lowndes County, Mississippi lawsuit, it was described as having "extensive business upon said 'Tom Bigbee' river and also upon the 'Black Warrior' river."

Emma Lou, sank at Columbus at the end of Main Street.

Emma Wattts, 111-ton side-wheeler built in 1851; during 1855–56 season it made two trips to Aberdeen; snagged Mobile, Alabama, 9/22/1858.

Empress, 304-ton side-wheeler built in 1850; 1,900-bale capacity or higher; burned, Algiers, Louisiana, 6/29/1859.

Era No. 9, stern-wheeler built in 1868 or 1869; Columbus trade, 1880.

Eureka, 110-ton side-wheeler built in 1845; 800-bale capacity or higher; Mobile-Columbus-Aberdeen packet spring 1846 and in 1847; snagged McNeil's Bar, Alabama, 11/6/1847.

Exchange, 67-ton side-wheeler built 1835; 400-bale capacity; abandoned 1843.

Express, Mobile–Columbus–Cotton Gin Port packet, January 1839.

Express No. 2, 59-ton side-wheeler built in 1837; exploded Blakely, Alabama, 7/25/1840, six lost.

Factor, 173-ton side-wheeler built in 1838; 1,000-bale capacity; Upper Tombigbee trade 1845–46; abandoned 1849.

Falls City, 183-ton stern-wheeler built in 1855; was the Wednesday evening packet from Mobile to Columbus and Aberdeen in 1859; foundered Loggy Bayou, Louisiana, 4/19/1864.

Fanny W., a small steamer "owned by Colored Men"; its boiler exploded seven miles north of Columbus, near Waverly, on 8/9/1878; there were eight to ten people on board, all of whom were severely injured.

Farmer, 198-ton side-wheeler built in 1848; 1,700-bale capacity; snagged Cairo, Illinois, 9/19/1859, three lives lost.

Farmer, 232-ton side-wheeler built in 1832; abandoned 1840.

Fashion, 296-ton side-wheeler built in 1851 in New Albany, Indiana; 2,000-bale capacity or higher; Upper Tombigbee River trade in 1856; Warrior

The bell from the steamer *Fashion* is located at the Missionary Union Baptist Church in Columbus, Mississippi.

River trade in 1857; abandoned 1857; bell is now at Missionary Union Baptist Church in Columbus.

Favorite, 158-ton side-wheeler built in 1837; 950-bale capacity; abandoned 1842.

Fleta, built in 1869 and in Upper Tombigbee trade in 1878–79; Columbus trade in 1880.

Flora, 118-ton side-wheeler built in 1835; abandoned 1844.

Forest Monarch, 215-ton side-wheeler built in 1848; 1,500-bale capacity; was Columbus mobile freight and passenger steamer in spring 1852; in Aberdeen and Columbus trade 1852–54; it was subject of an 1852 court action for transporting a runaway slave in case no. 8799 of the Lowndes County Circuit Court; snagged Tombigbee River near Pickensville 4/14/1855 (or 1853); it was still on the Tombigbee in 1855.

Fox, 91-ton side-wheeler built in 1834; 500-bale capacity; Cotton Gin Port trade 1836–37; snagged Mobile, Alabama, 8/6/1840.

Frank Lyon, 446-ton side-wheeler built in 1851; 1,900-bale capacity; reported abandoned 1857 but in the Tombigbee/Warrior trade in 1859.

Frank S. Stone, 247-ton built in 1897; it was in the Mobile-Vienna-Columbus trade from 1898 to 1902; it left Vienna for Mobile eight days before it capsized and sank, 27 Mile Bluff, Mobile River, 1/2/1902.

Friendship, in the Columbus trade.

Fulton, 206-ton side-wheeler built in 1852; 1,200-bale capacity or higher; lost 1863.

Gainesville, 221-ton side-wheeler built in 1839; collided Mobile, Alabama, 3/31/1843.

Gem, flatboat built in 1884; 400-bale capacity.

General R.E. Lee, built in 1862; made three trips to Columbus during 1862–63 season.

General Sumpter, 160-ton side-wheeler built in 1835; 1,000-bale capacity or higher; abandoned 1843; Columbus trade 1835–36 season.

General Taylor, 119-ton side-wheeler built in 1846; Judge Foster described it as "a neat little packet...brought to Mobile to run on the Tombigbee in the interest of the Columbus and Aberdeen trade"; abandoned 1852.

General William H. Harrison, 63-ton side-wheeler built in 1839; 1,000-bale capacity or higher; abandoned 1846; in 1846, lawsuit; all that remained of the boat were three boilers and two chimneys, and the britching was seized.

General W.S. Hancock, 174-ton stern-wheeler built in 1880; the name was changed to *W.H. Gardner*.

mh7 82tds   C. BANCROFT, Sheriff M. C.

District Court of the United States—Mobile.
James Martin
vs.
The Steamboat General Harrison.

BY virtue of a writ of seizure to me directed in the above entitled cause, I have seized and taken into my possession so much of the said Steamboat as I can find, to wit: three Boilers, two Chimneys and britching. All persons having or pretending to have claim to said boilers, chimneys and britching, are cited to appear at the term of the District Court to be held on the first Monday of April next, at the Court House of the United States in the city of Mobile, there and then to shew cause if any they can whereof the said boilers, chimneys, &c. shall not be condemned to the use of the libelant.   [mh25 95]   J. G. LYON, U. S. M.

SALT—3000 bleached sacks. per ship Schoodiac, for sale in the Bay or on the wharf by

A legal notice from a Mobile newspaper in 1845 on the steamer *General Harrison*.

Georgia Sykes, side-wheeler built in 1860 for the Aberdeen trade; Aberdeen and Columbus trade 1861 and 1862; Pickensville and Moore's Bluff trade in March 1863.

Gopher, 98.7-ton stern-wheeler built in 1895; it was 84.5 feet by 22.7 by 4.5 feet; Clarence B. Moore's steamer that he used during his archaeological survey of the "Little Tombigbee River" for the Academy of Natural Science, Philadelphia, in 1900–1901.

Gov. Israel Pickens, 218-ton side-wheeler built in 1837; 1,100-bale capacity or higher; abandoned 1846.

Grand Bay, built in 1857 and owned by Aberdeen interest; Upper Tombigbee trade in 1858.

Hale, 134-ton stern-wheeler built in 1869; 600-bale capacity or higher; sank Tombigbee River, date unknown; Upper Tombigbee trade in 1874, 1875, 1879 and 1880.

Hale, see *James L. Hale*, 1913.

The steamers *Gopher* and *Vienna* at Columbus in 1901.

Left: The steamer *Hard Cash* and an unidentified steamer at the Mobile Wharf, circa 1900.

Below: A waybill from the steamer *Hattie B. Moore* for goods carried up the Tombigbee from Mobile to Pickensville, Alabama, in 1887.

Hard Cash, stern-wheeler built in 1876; Tombigbee trade in 1889; in Columbus trade in 1890s through 1912; it used the barges *Nyanza* and *Mattie Belle* during the 1890s; in 1903, its captain, Tom Bartee, was arrested at the Columbus wharf for illegally selling whiskey on the *Hard Cash*; it was dismantled at Mobile in 1914.

Harriet, 42-ton side-wheeler built in 1821, with a fifteen-horsepower engine; it was the first steamboat to Montgomery on 10/21/1821; Upper Tombigbee trade in 1826; it burst its boilers at Coffeeville on 2/6/1827, killing one person.

Hattie Belle, 57-ton stern-wheeler built in 1885 for Aberdeen lumber trade.

Hattie B. Moore, stern-wheeler built in 1883; in Mobile-Pickensville trade in 1887; destroyed in Mobile hurricane of 1906.

Helen Burk, built in 1914 as the *Peerless* using the hull, two boilers and machinery of the *James T. Staples*; it was renamed in 1924; Forkland trade in the 1920s.

Helen, 292-ton side-wheeler built in 1850; 1,800-bale capacity or higher; known as "Little Helen"; caught fire near Moore's Bluff in 1854 and was sunk by its crew to put out the fire and then was raised; in Upper Tombigbee trade 1853–54; it burned at Mobile, Alabama, on 5/12/1855.

H. Kinney (*Henderson Kinney*), 130-ton side-wheeler built in 1844; 900-bale capacity or higher; it was built in for the Aberdeen trade; while bound for Aberdeen, it exploded at Wilkins Landing, Tombigbee River, 5/28/1848; reports stated seventeen lives lost; Lloyd's list gives a date of 6/5/1848 for the explosion and states that fifty crew and passengers killed.

Herald, 135-ton side-wheeler built in 1825; 1,200-barrel capacity; 500-bale capacity; collided with *Helen McGregor*, Mobile, Alabama, 12/23/1832.

Herald, 205-ton side-wheeler built in 1832; abandoned 1836.

Heroine, 94-ton stern-wheeler built in 1851; 437-bale capacity; exploded at Blakely, Alabama, 3/13/1855, three lives lost in one report, eight in another.

Hewitt, probably the *James Hewitt*, Mobile-Columbus, four trips during 1850–51 season.

Holt, see *William S. Holt*.

Hugh L. White, 175-ton side-wheeler built in 1839; collapsed a flue below Demopolis, one died; burned at St. Louis, Missouri, 5/20/1850.

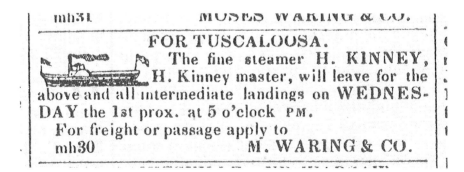

An 1846 advertisement from the *Mobile Register* for the steamer *H. Kinney*.

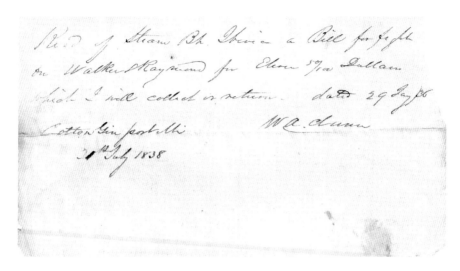

A waybill from the steamer *Iberia* at Cotton Gin Port, Mississippi, in 1838.

Hunter, 149-ton side-wheeler built in 1832; Tombigbee trade in 1833; burned at Jones Bluff, Tombigbee River, 4/12/1836 or 6/15/1836; 190 bales of cotton were lost.

Iberia, 136-ton side-wheeler built in 1834; in 1836 it was partly owned by Columbus interest; in Columbus and Cotton Gin Port trade 1835–36; it was in the Hamilton, Mississippi trade in 1837 and in the Mobile-Columbus trade in 1839; it was the subject of a lawsuit in Columbus over lost cargo in case no. 202 of the Lowndes County Circuit Court.

Illinois Belle, 143-ton stern-wheeler built in 1854; abandoned 1859.

India, side-wheeler built in 1842; 1,500-bale capacity or higher.

Iowa, 143-ton side-wheeler built in 1834; 600-bale capacity; burned Fairfield, Tombigbee River, 1/17/1837 or 1/19/1837, no lives lost.

Irene, 76-ton side-wheeler built in 1844; it ran between Camargo and West Port during 1847–48 season; its cotton would be loaded onto a flatboat at West Port to await shipment by a larger steamer to Mobile; lost at Mobile 4/1/1850.

Isabella, 249-ton side-wheeler built in 1849; 1,622-bale capacity or higher; burned 2/1/1860.

Isora, 124-ton side-wheeler built in 1839; 702-bale capacity or higher; snagged Craig's Ferry, Alabama, 4/30/1842.

Itawamba, a barge built in 1909.

Jack Downey, on the Tombigbee in 1835.

Jack Downing, 99-ton side-wheeler built in 1844; 557-bale capacity or higher; abandoned 1837.

Jackson, 47-ton stern-wheel towboat built in during late 1890s; it was 102.2 feet by 22.2 by 2.4 feet; it was probably the *Jackson* that twice carried cotton from Vienna to Demopolis in December 1901; it was rebuilt and renamed the *Swan* and was owned by a lumber mill at Eppes; in 1920 it ran aground and broke up above Gainesville.

James Dellet, 195-ton side-wheeler built in 1859; snagged Gardner's Island, 7/26/1862; Columbus trade March 1862; Pickensville trade February 1862.

James Hewett, 336-ton side-wheeler built in 1843; 3,500-bale capacity; rescued the survivors of the *Tuscaloosa* north of Mobile on 1/29/1847; it was a fast steamer that could run from Mobile to Demopolis in eighteen to nineteen hours; it foundered at Carondelet, Missouri, 8/18/1851.

James L. Hale, 60-ton stern-wheeler built in 1909 for Red River; it was bought by Baker Towing Company, Tuscaloosa, in 1912; arrived in Columbus 2/18/1913, and then left for Aberdeen on the nineteenth; it was sold to Demopolis Lumber Company and later converted to diesel; often called the *Hale*, it was still being operated by the lumber company on the Lower Tombigbee in 1955.

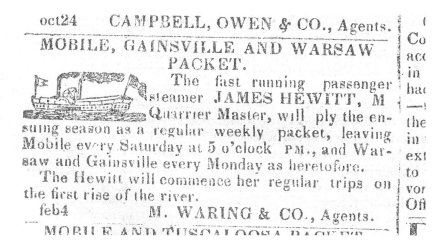

An 1846 advertisement from the *Mobile Register* for the steamer *James Hewett*.

James T. Staples; see *Helen Burk*.

Jeanette, 144-ton stern-wheeler built in 1854; abandoned 1857; Gainesville trade November 1859.

Jennie Bealle, 231-ton side-wheeler built in 1852; 1,800-bale capacity or higher; made four trips to Aberdeen during 1855–56 season; abandoned 1859.

Jenny Lind, 77-ton side-wheeler built in 1850; 1,450-bale capacity or higher; made nineteen trips to Columbus during 1850–51 season, the last being on May 13; on 2/21/1851, loaded 1,100 bales of cotton at West Port during a flood—largest shipment from one warehouse on the Upper Tombigbee at one time; abandoned 1865.

J.E. Roberts, side-wheeler built in 1844; 770-bale capacity.

Jim, 55-ton stern-wheeler built about 1845; 437-bale capacity or higher; abandoned 1850.

J.L. Webb, built before 1850.

John Briggs, 352-ton side-wheeler built in 1856; 1,820-bale capacity or higher; West Port and Aberdeen, January 1860; Columbus trade, 1865–66; abandoned 1868.

John D. Moore, built in 1900.

John Duncan, 215-ton side-wheeler built in 1839; snagged at Tuscaloosa, Alabama, 12/30/1844.

An 1860 waybill from the steamer *John Briggs*.

John Quill, 270-ton stern-wheeler built in 1907 in Jefferson, Indiana; it was 168' by 35' by 4.9'; in August 1908 it was the Tuesday and Saturday Mobile packet for Demopolis; it was in the Columbus trade in 1912; on 1/9/1913, it rescued survivors of the *James T. Staples*; on 6/12/1916, it sank after striking a rock in the Warrior River but was raised; it sank in the Mobile River at Twelve Mile Island in 1929.

John T. Moore, 457-ton stern-wheeler, iron hull built in 1871; it may have been the steamer *Moore* that made a trip to Columbus in January 1878 and in January 1879; it was sold to Mississippi River, where it was renamed the *Endeaver* during 1880s.

John W. Russell, 138-ton side-wheeler built in 1848; abandoned 1852.

Julia, side-wheeler built in 1852.

Juniatta, 110-ton side-wheeler built in 1832; 450-bale capacity or higher; snagged at Mobile, Alabama, 10/11/1842.

Kansas, 111-ton side-wheeler built in 1836; 754-bale capacity or higher; Columbus trade spring of 1840 and Cotton Gin Port trade in 1840; exploded at Claiborne, Alabama, 11/4/1841.

Lady Monroe, keelboat; Cotton Gin Port–Mobile trade, 1821–22.

Lallah Roohk, 156-ton stern-wheeler built in 1838; 900-bale capacity or higher; Upper Tombigbee trade, 1839–42; abandoned 1847.

Lawrence, Columbus trade in 1867; the steamer *Virginia No. 1* with the barge or flatboat *Lawrence* transported 200 bales of cotton to Mobile for James Sykes of Columbus.

Le Compte, 288-ton side-wheeler built in 1855; 2,000-bale capacity; made eleven trips to Aberdeen during 1855–56 season; Aberdeen trade, December 1859; burned Mobile, Alabama, 3/27/1861.

Leo, 343-ton side-wheeler built in 1863 (or 1868); it was the weekly Mobile-Columbus packet in January 1875 and would land at the foot of Main Street in Columbus; sold to Rio Grande River in 1875 and destroyed there by a hurricane in 1880.

Leona, 232-ton side-wheeler built in 1856; 2,000-bale capacity; snagged 12/16/1859, Coushatta, Louisiana.

Lewis Cass, 111-ton side-wheeler built in 1835; 800-bale capacity or higher; abandoned 1842.

Liberty, stern-wheeler built in 1889; 164 by 34.4 by 5 feet; it was sold to Mobile interest as a Tombigbee packet in 1902; sold to Alabama Towing

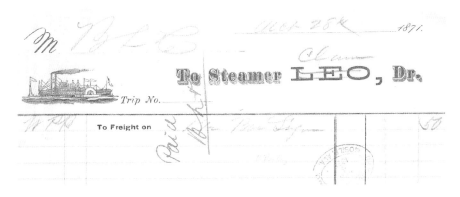

A form waybill for the steamer *Leo* changed to steamer *Clara* on the Alabama River in 1871.

Company for the Montgomery-Selma-Mobile trade in 1910; its Texas deck was removed, and it was used as towboat; in 1912 it was sold to a Pittsburg, Pennsylvania interest and was rebuilt by them and renamed the *City of Parkersburg*; it sank at Russell, Kentucky, in 1918.

Lillie Lou, 58-ton side-wheeler built in Monroe County in 1878 or '79; 600-bale capacity; it was built in by Aberdeen interest along with a barge, the *Maggie Virginia*, to access trade on small streams for Aberdeen markets; Columbus trade 1879; Aberdeen-Fulton trade 1880–81 season; on trip from Mobile to Macon snagged and sank on the Noxubee in 1883 but was raised and refloated.

Lily, 159-ton stern-wheeler built in 1860 and sank in May 1863 but was raised and used to transport Confederate artillery from Columbus to Mobile in January 1865; in 1865 it was described as "the little steamer Lily" by a Confederate officer.

Little Corporal, 22-ton built circa 1878 for F.M. Leigh and Company of Columbus; in February 1880 it struck a snag and sank twenty-five miles below Columbus; it was raised and returned to Columbus trade; it later burned.

Little Harriet, 47-ton side-wheeler built in 1843; snagged at Mobile, Alabama, 8/2/1849.

Little Rock, 84-ton side-wheeler built in 1832; abandoned 1838.

Lotus No. 2, 230-ton stern-wheeler built in 1866; 562-bale capacity or higher; Friday packet Mobile–Pickensville–Moore's Bluff–Columbus 1875; 1877–1880 Pickensville–Great Southern Railroad packet; Billups and

The steamer *Little Corporal* at the Tombigbee Landing in Columbus during the 1880s.

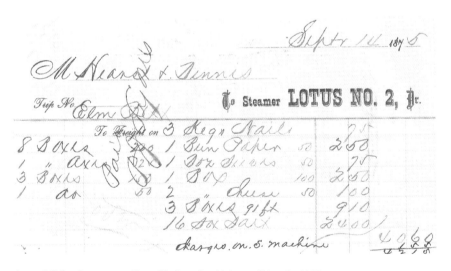

A waybill for the steamer *Lotus No. 2* on the Alabama River in 1875.

Banks were Columbus agents in 1882; on the Upper Tombigbee 1887; it was destroyed by a storm in 1893 in Mobile.

Louisa, 393-ton side-wheeler built in 1851; 2,313-bale capacity or higher; snagged Harrisonburg, Louisiana, 3/2/1855.

Louisa Hopkins, 210-ton side-wheeler built in 1846; 1,000-bale capacity; abandoned 1852.

Lowndes, 229-ton side-wheeler built in 1844; 1,605-bale capacity or higher; Mobile-Columbus trade 1848–49; abandoned 1856.

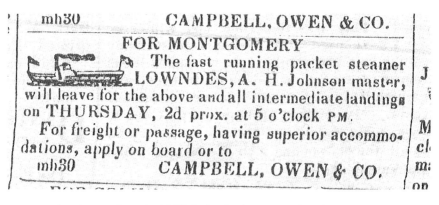

An 1846 advertisement from the *Mobile Register* for the steamer *Lowndes*.

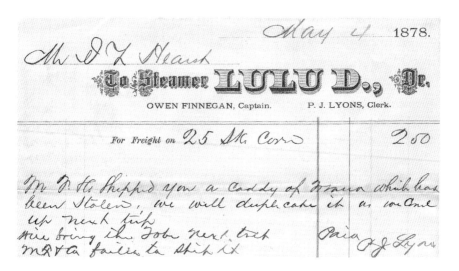

A waybill from the steamer *Lulu D.* on the Alabama River in 1878.

Lucy Bell, 169-ton side-wheeler built in 1853; 1,202-bale capacity or higher; Upper Tombigbee trade in 1854; made two trips to Aberdeen during 1855–56 season; abandoned 1859.

Lucy Robinson, 239-ton side-wheeler built in 1851; 1,257-bale capacity or higher; abandoned 1859.

Lulu D., 245-ton stern-wheeler built in 1867; Tuesday packet, Pickensville and Columbus 1874 and 1875; Columbus trade 1874–79; abandoned 1885.

Madison, 169-ton built in 1852; 11,449-bale capacity or higher; one trip to Aberdeen 1855–56 season; collided Aurora, Indiana, 1859.

Maggie C., 93-ton stern-wheeler built circa 1874; Columbus trade 1875.

Maggie Calhoun, stern-wheeler; Pickensville trade, December 1873; left Columbus for Mobile carrying 200 bales of cotton from Columbus and 400 from Aberdeen on 1/24/1874; may be same boat as *Maggie C*, as both were in Moore's Bluff trade in 1874.

Maggie Virginia, a barge built circa 1878; 200-bale capacity.

Magnolia, 325-ton side-wheeler built in 1852; 1,400-bale capacity or higher; in a collision with the steamer Maluka on the Alabama River, 2/16/1854, three died; in 1859, it was the Tuesday evening packet from Mobile to Vienna and Warsaw on the Upper Tombigbee and Pickensville–Upper Tombigbee trade, 1863–64 season; it carried the survivors of the *Eliza Battle* disaster to Mobile in 1858; it sank at Selma in 1867.

Marengo, 158-ton side-wheeler built in 1856; 309-bale capacity or higher; Columbus trade 1865–66; abandoned 1867.

A waybill from the steamer *Maggie Calhoun* in the Upper Tombigbee trade in January 1874.

A waybill from the steamer *Magnolia* for goods shipped from Mobile to Demopolis in 1860.

Marietta, 139-ton built in 1825; 465-bale capacity or higher; Mobile-Columbus trade 1831–32; on one trip from Hamilton on the Upper Tombigbee to Mobile in 1832, it carried 465 bales of cotton, 37 bales of deerskins, 1,300 bales of cowhide, a box of furs and five barrels of beeswax; abandoned 1839.

Marquette, 126-ton side-wheeler built in 1842; 874-bale capacity or higher; exploded New Orleans, Louisiana, 7/1/1845, thirteen lives lost.

Mary Bess, 206-ton side-wheeler built in 1852; 1,357-bale capacity or higher; abandoned 1858.

Mary Boyd, 383-ton built in 1869; Tuesday packet for Vienna in 1882 or 1883.

Mary Conley, 161-ton side-wheeler built in 1865; 750-bale capacity or higher; Aberdeen-Columbus trade, fall 1866 to the spring of 1868; in February 1867, it carried 1 bale of cotton to Mobile from Moore's Bluff for James Sykes of Columbus, and the freight charge was $3.50; it was lost in 1871.

Mary Elizabeth, stern-wheeler built in 1877; 500-bale capacity.

Mary Glover, built circa 1867 (could also be *Molly Glover*).

Mary M., 59-ton stern-wheel; regular Columbus packet, 1891; later renamed *Sipsey*; Pickensville trade 1891; sold to U.S. Army Corps of Engineers in 1891.

A waybill from the steamer *Mary Conley* for goods shipped up river from Mobile in 1869.

The steamers *Mary S. Blees* and *Vienna* at Demopolis circa 1905.

Mary S. Blees, 214-ton stern-wheeler built in 1899; its hull was 170 feet by 34 feet by 4.5 feet; in 1908, it was the Staples Lines Mobile to Demopolis packet; sold to Ohio River in 1916 and renamed *Piase*.

Mattie B. Moore, Tombigbee trade in 1889.

Medora, 210-ton side-wheeler built in 1835; 1,500-bale capacity or higher; Mobile-Columbus trade, 1841; snagged at McGrew's Shoals, 11/22/1842.

A waybill from the steamer *Mist* on the Alabama River in 1871.

Meridian, 195-ton side-wheeler built in 1836; 1,083-bale capacity or higher; Aberdeen-Columbus trade in 1841; abandoned 1842.

Minerva, 850-bale capacity or higher.

Mist, 232-ton stern-wheeler built in 1864; 545-bale capacity or higher; Columbus-Aberdeen trade 1865–67; it sank at Frank Earls Shoals, Alabama River, 1874.

Molly Glover, made one trip to Columbus during the 1866–67 season.

Monroe, 70-ton built in 1826; abandoned 1829.

Montana, 231-ton side-wheeler built in 1865; Upper Tombigbee trade in 1868; abandoned 1872.

Motive, 67-ton stern-wheeler built in 1845; 335-bale capacity or higher; broke up on sandbar south of Barton, 2/27/1850.

National, 379-ton built in 1860; Tuesday packet for Pickensville, December 1870; abandoned 1873.

Native, 136-ton side-wheeler built in 1841; 901-bale capacity or higher; Mobile-Columbus trade, 1846; Mobile–Cotton Gin Port trade in 1841 to 1847, including five trips in the spring of 1842; abandoned 1872.

Nettie Quill, 299-ton stern-wheeler built in 1896; its hull was 178 feet by 33 feet by 5.5 feet; moved to New Orleans in 1914; renamed *Monroe* and destroyed by storm in 1915.

MOBILE & COLUMBUS REGULAR WEEKLY PACKET.

The fine and fast running passenger steamer NEW ERA, Joe H. Estes, master, will ply as a regular weekly packet in the above trade during the season, leaving Mobile every TUESDAY, at 5 o'clock P M.

The N. E. will commence her trips with first rise of water.

oct24   CAMPBELL, OWEN & CO., Agents.

MOBILE, GAINSVILLE AND WARSAW

An 1846 advertisement from the *Mobile Register* for the steamer *New Era*.

New Albany, 903-bale capacity or higher; was weekly Pickensville-Columbus packet in 1843.

New Era, 246-ton built circa 1843; 1,228-bale capacity; in November 1845, advertised as "fast running passenger steamer," leaving Mobile every Tuesday for Columbus; Thursday packet Mobile–West Port–Columbus, 1846; Columbus-Mobile in 1848.

New Haven, 92-ton stern-wheeler built in 1882; 500-bale capacity; it was bought for the Columbus trade by J.E. Stewart in December 1908 to replace the larger steamer *American*, which had been sold to Alabama River interest; it was still in the Columbus trade in 1909; it snagged and sank near Demopolis, Alabama, in 1910; its wreck was later burned.

New World, 246-ton side-wheeler built in 1843; 1,068-bale capacity or higher; a fast boat that could make Mobile to Demopolis in eighteen to nineteen hours; Columbus trade in 1847; abandoned 1848.

Niagara, 125-ton side-wheeler built in 1836; 958-bale capacity or higher; Columbus trade in the spring of 1841; collided at Montgomery, Alabama, 12/10/1841, ten lives lost.

Niobara, stern-wheeler built circa 1884.

Noah's Ark, large flatboat built in 1879.

Norfolk, 219-ton side-wheeler built in 1838; 681-bale capacity or higher; snagged at Mobile, 7/2/1849.

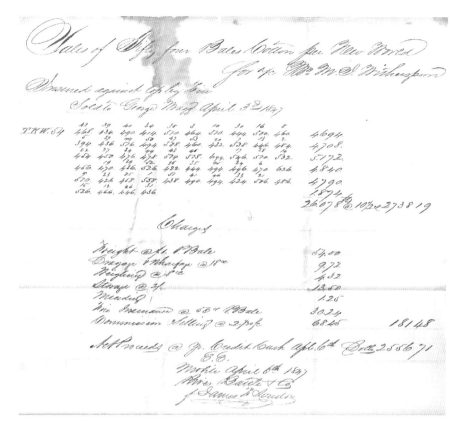

An accounting—including number and weight of cotton bales—of cotton shipped from Lowndes County, Mississippi, to Mobile on the steamer *New World* in 1847.

Norma, 188-ton side-wheeler built in 1839; 700-barrel capacity; 872-bale capacity or higher; Wednesday packet Mobile-Columbus-Plymouth, 1843; snagged at Mobile, Alabama, 6/1/1846.

North Alabama, side-wheeler built in 1844; 982-bale capacity or higher.

Noxubee, 108-ton side-wheeler built in 1842; 700-bale capacity; abandoned 1850.

Nyanza, barge used by *Hard Cash* in 1890s; was remains of steamer *Nyanza*; dismantled in 1873.

Octavia, 185-ton side-wheeler built in 1852; 981-bale capacity; abandoned 1859.

Olive, 115-ton side-wheeler built in 1847; 725-bale capacity; in 1850 it was the first steamboat to Fulton; 1848–51 it was in the Fulton and Camargo trade.

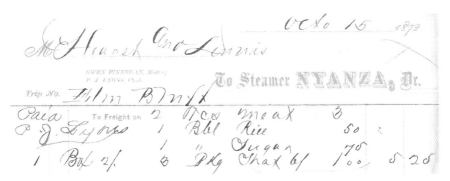

A waybill from the *Nyanza* from when it was operating as a steamboat.

The steamer *Ouachita* on the Tombigbee circa 1905.

Ophelia, 113-ton side-wheeler built in 1832; 400-bale capacity or higher; snagged but raised near Tuscaloosa in 1837; Columbus-Aberdeen trade in 1838 and was the first boat of that season to reach Columbus and Aberdeen; snagged and lost below Tuscaloosa in late March or April 1838.

Oriole, 110-ton side-wheeler built in 1840; 605-bale capacity or higher; sold away in 1846.

Ouachita, 99-ton stern-wheeler built in 1899; Columbus trade, 1905–6; dismantled in 1909 at Mobile, Alabama.

Ozark, built circa 1840; 826-bale capacity.

Pascagoula, built circa 1847; 377-bale capacity or higher.

P.C. Wallace, 230-ton side-wheeler built in 1855; 1,421-bale capacity or higher; Upper Tombigbee trade in 1856; passed to Confederate control in 1861 (could also be *P.C. Wallis*).

Peerless, see *Helen Burk.*

Penelope, 121-ton side-wheeler built in 1842; 516-bale capacity or higher; burned at Mobile on 10/15/1846.

Picayune, 48-ton stern-wheeler built in 1846; 453-bale capacity; Columbus trade in 1841; abandoned 1851.

Pink Toney, 206-ton side-wheeler built in 1852; 2,000-bale capacity; during 1856–57 season it made one trip to Camargo and carried off 1,055 bales of cotton; made four trips to Aberdeen during 1855–56 season; foundered at sea 7/28/1858.

Piny Woods, Warsaw-Mobile packet in May 1864.

Pioneer, 139-ton side-wheeler built in 1835; 1,015-bale capacity; Mobile-Columbus 1839; sold away in 1844.

Planter, 116-ton side-wheeler built in 1831; 635-bale capacity or higher; lost 1836.

Planter, a steamer by this name arrived at the Columbus wharf on 1/24/1874.

Ploughboy, 142-ton side-wheeler built in 1834; 1,157-bale capacity; made four trips to Cotton Gin Port in 1834–35; snagged at Mobile, Alabama, 1/14/1839, having departed Columbus 1/9/1839.

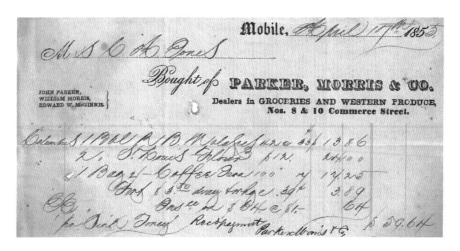

Goods shipped to Columbus from Mobile on the steamer *Pink Toney* in 1855.

A letter carried from Demopolis to Selma, Alabama, by the steamer *Prairie State* in 1869.

Ponchartrain, 132-ton side-wheeler built in 1834; 622-bale capacity or higher; one trip to Cotton Gin Port 1836–37 season; abandoned 1841.

Post Boy, listed by Rodabough as built circa 1854 and in Columbus trade in 1854; it is not included in an 1855–56 list of Mobile steamboats.

Potomac, 198-ton side-wheeler built in 1844; 1,450-bale capacity; stranded at Galveston, Texas, 7/1/1846.

Prairie State, 184-ton built in Wellsville, Ohio; on Mobile River in 1863; Mobile-Livingston, Alabama trip post 1865; Demopolis trade in 1869; abandoned 1872.

Putnam, 190-ton side-wheeler built in 1845; 775-bale capacity; Cotton Gin Port trade 1847–48 season; stranded Ten Mile Shoals, Little Tombigbee River, 2/13/1848.

Queen of the South, 208-ton side-wheeler built in 1841; 1,169-bale capacity or higher; Columbus trade during the spring of 1843; snagged at Island No. 34, 8/3/1842.

Quincy, a flatboat from Martin's Bluff that wrecked in 1848 while carrying cotton to Mobile; the steamer *Young Renown* salvaged 178 bales of cotton from it.

Rainbow, built in 1848; 560-bale capacity or higher.

Rambler, 118-ton side-wheeler built in 1823; abandoned 1830.

Reindeer, 360-ton side-wheeler built in 1860; made two trips to Columbus in 1862–63 season.

Reindeer, 267-ton side-wheeler built in 1865; 1,446-bale capacity; Columbus and Aberdeen trade 1865–68; it had a calliope, and when near Columbus, children would run to the M&O bridge to watch it and listen; Wyatt recalled, "On its top deck was a large wooden deer kept painted in the proper color and it carried a calliope; the most remarkable thing about it, however, was its whistle which made a weird wild scream like some distressed animal lost from its fellows"; abandoned 1874.

R.E. Lee, 233-ton built in 1873; Pickensville trade January 1890; abandoned 1890s.

Renown, built circa 1841; 682-bale capacity; arrived in Columbus 1/15/1841, after four days from Mobile; snagged below Moore's Bluff, 2/24/1841.

Rescue, 76-ton built in 1854.

Rescue, 207-ton built in 1854; Mobile-Warsaw packet in 1860; snagged at Tompkin's Bluff December 1860.

Reserve, 115-ton side-wheeler built in 1837; 638-bale capacity or higher; stranded at Tompkin's Bluff, Alabama, 5/14/1842.

Reveille, stern-wheeler; ran from Camargo to Columbus during the 1848–49 season.

A waybill from the steamer *Reindeer* in 1872. This was the second steamer by that name on the Tombigbee.

Roanoke, 262-ton side-wheeler built in 1835; 965-bale capacity or higher; Mobile-Columbus trade spring 1839 and 1841; stranded at Woods Bluff, Alabama, 1/23/1842, one life lost.

Robert Bailey, a flatboat that carried 28 bales of cotton from Hamilton to Mobile in May 1830.

Robert Morris, 123-ton side-wheeler built in 1835; 578-bale capacity or higher; abandoned 1842.

Robert Watson, 137-ton built in 1855; abandoned 1871; Mobile-Gainesville trade May 1864.

Rome, built about 1850.

Romeo, 140-ton side-wheeler built in 1850; 859-bale capacity; Mobile-Columbus-Aberdeen trade, fall 1850; it made twelve trips to Columbus during 1850–51 season; on 2/17/1851, it attempted to pass under the bridge at Columbus while the river was at a high flood stage; it lost its pilothouse and wheelhouse; snagged at Campagnolle, Arkansas, 12/31/1851.

Ruby, built circa 1855; 741-bale capacity; made one trip to Aberdeen during 1855–56 season.

Ruby, 98-ton side-wheeler built in 1843; 633-bale capacity or higher; bound for Aberdeen, it was struck by *Red Rover* at Fort Stoddard, Alabama, 3/9/1845; its cabin broke free and floated from the hull, which sank; it was towed to shore by *Red Rover*, saving many lives, though two were lost.

Ruth, 181-ton side-wheeler built in 1870; 1,000-bale capacity; Upper Tombigbee trade in 1879; Tuesday packet for Vienna in the spring of 1883.

Sallie Carson, 206-ton stern-wheeler built in 1852; 1,771-bale capacity; it made eleven trips to Aberdeen during 1855–56 season; Judge Foster described it as "a very pretty, trimly built in craft"; abandoned 1858.

Sallie Spann, 190-ton side-wheeler built in 1852; 2,383-bale capacity; Mobile-Columbus-Aberdeen trade 1852–53 season; burned at Mobile, Alabama, 11/22/1856.

Sarah, built circa 1850; 875-bale capacity or higher; it was the Monday Mobile-Columbus packet in 1851–52 and 1852–53; it would leave Mobile Monday night and arrive in Columbus Wednesday night; it was refitted and painted in September 1851.

Selma, 320-ton side-wheeler built in 1856; 1,614-bale capacity or higher; Columbus trade November 1859; passed to Confederate control but

FOR COLUMBUS & WAVERLY.
THE new and magnificent
swift passenger steamer

S. S. PRENTISS,

GID B. MASSEY, Master.
J. P. COATS, Clerk.

Having been purchased expressly for the
abovetrade, will commence her regular trips
so soon asthe navigation opens permanently
in the Bigbee River, and continue through
the season, leaving Mobile every **WED-
NESDAY**, at 5 o'clock, P. M., punctually, and Columbus every **SATURDAY**,
at 9 o'clock, A. M., and arrive in Mobile on
Friday mornings.

☞The Prentiss classes No. 1, in the Insurance offices, and will run entirely **INDE-
PENDENT** of anyother boat or company.

Feb. 7, 1856. 1-6m

A clipping from an 1856 Columbus, Mississippi newspaper advertising the *S.S. Prentiss*.

captured 8/5/1864; redocumented 8/17/1865; foundered off mouth of Brazos River, Texas, 6/24/1868, six lives lost.

Selma, 227-ton side-wheeler built in 1845; 995-bale capacity or higher; collided with *D.B. Mosby* at Cahawba, Alabama, 5/29/1850.

Senator No. 2, 295-ton side-wheeler built in 1858; 1,800-bale capacity; sank at Young Landing, Alabama River, 1870s.

Shylock, 180-ton side-wheeler built in 1837; 1,025-bale capacity; Columbus-Aberdeen trade 1841; abandoned 1843.

Southerner, 298-ton side-wheeler built in 1836; 1,211-bale capacity; it was described as having "a double engine"; Columbus trade 1841; grounded at Ten Mile Shoals on the Little Tombigbee in 1843; snagged at New Orleans, Louisiana, 5/21/1851.

Southern Trader, keelboat; Columbus-Mobile, 1820.

S.S. Prentiss, 272-ton side-wheeler built in 1853; 1,226-bale capacity; Upper Tombigbee trade 1855–57; it was known as a swift boat; burned at Algiers, Louisiana, 2/20/1859.

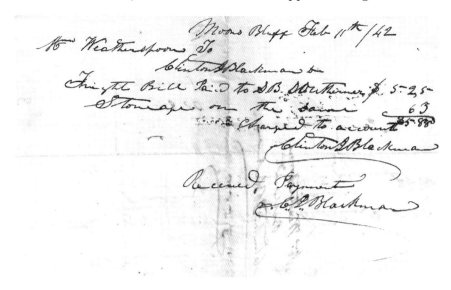

Goods shipped to Moore's Bluff, on the Tombigbee below Columbus, by the steamer *Southerner* in 1842.

Sun, 136-ton side-wheeler built in 1821; 872-bale capacity; Upper Tombigbee trade 1833–35; snagged at Mobile, Alabama, 8/6/1840.

Sunny South, 196-ton side-wheeler built in 1847; 1,258-bale capacity or higher; Mobile-Columbus packet 1849–50; it made eleven trips to Columbus during the 1850–51 season; snagged at Mobile, Alabama, 10/1/1855.

Susie B., built circa 1883.

Swiss Boy, 121-ton side-wheeler built in 1835; 1,222-bale capacity; abandoned 1844.

Tallapoosa, 124-ton side-wheeler built in 1836; 589-bale capacity or higher; abandoned 1842.

Tally, Columbus trade in 1887 (may be *D.L. Tally*).

Telegraph, 165-ton side-wheeler built in 1840; 814-bale capacity; sold to the War Department, 1846.

Tiger, 333-ton side-wheeler built in 1858; 1,780-bale capacity; Columbus–West Port packet in 1859; snagged at Alexandria, Louisiana, 4/2/1860.

Tolby, stern-wheeler built circa 1900.

Triumph, 68-ton side-wheeler built in 1837; 395-bale capacity; sank on Tombigbee near junction with Alabama in 1837 but was raised; in the Mobile-Columbus trade 1838–39; one trip to Cotton Gin Port also in 1839; abandoned 1843.

Tropic, 123-ton side-wheeler built in 1836; 1,259-bale capacity; in 1836–37 it was owned by Columbus interest, including Richard Barry as part owner; William Cooper was "first cook" from January 17 to May 1, 1837, with wages of sixty-five dollars per month; failure to pay wages was the subject of a Lowndes County, Mississippi Circuit Court action in case no. 3780; it was a Mobile-Columbus packet in 1840; abandoned 1843.

Turner, built circa 1847.

Tuscaloosa, 83-ton side-wheeler built in 1824; Upper Tombigbee trade 1826; abandoned 1826.

Tuscaloosa, ran on the Tombigbee and Warrior Rivers in 1859.

Tuscumbia, 215-ton side-wheeler built in 1826; 372-bale capacity or higher; snagged 12/2/1836.

Twining, built in 1883.

Union, 168-ton stern-wheeler built in 1845; 1,100-bale capacity; in 1846 was Mobile–Columbus–Waverly–Aberdeen–Cotton Gin Port packet; abandoned 1855.

Victoria, 179-ton side-wheeler built in 1838; 3,000-bale capacity; it had fourteen staterooms in the gentlemen's cabin and eight berths in the ladies' cabin; it was in the Mobile-Columbus trade in the spring of 1839

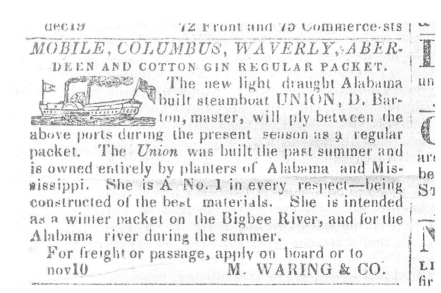

An 1845 advertisement from the *Mobile Register* for the steamer *Union*.

A waybill for the Tombigbee steamer *Victoria* in 1873.

and the spring of 1841; arrived in Columbus on 1/13/1841, after five days from Mobile; abandoned 1855.

Victoria, 191-ton stern-wheeler built in early 1870s; it was the "regular Saturday evening independent packet" to Demopolis in 1873.

Vienna, a snag boat active in 1911.

Vienna, 176-ton stern-wheeler built in 1898; 155 feet by 26 feet by 4.5 feet; it was built in for the Columbus-Mobile trade; it sank at Moore's Bluff, Ten Mile Shoals, Upper Tombigbee, on 1/19/1906, after hitting a "dead head" (sunken log); it was bound for Columbus and carrying 250 bales of cotton and 2,200 sacks of cottonseed.

Vigo, 144-ton side-wheeler built in 1859; 786-bale capacity or higher; abandoned 1868.

Vincennes, 95-ton side-wheeler built in 1833; 549-bale capacity or higher; was in the Mobile-Plymouth trade November 1833 to May 1834; Captain Leech of Columbus was its master and part owner, 1833–34; on 3/7/1834, it left Mobile and arrived at Plymouth at 11:00 p.m. on March 14; snagged at Mobile, Alabama, 2/10/1838; this steamer was the subject of a lawsuit in 1834, and the case file is in the county records in the Billups-Garth Archives, Columbus-Lowndes Public Library.

Viola, 156-ton side-wheeler built in 1843; 1,021-bale capacity; abandoned 1847.

Viola, small steamer leased by Gainesville, Alabama interest in February 1887 to run from Mobile to Gainesville to Macon; it probably only made one trip to Macon, as it was unsuccessful in obtaining a load of Noxubee cotton for shipment to Mobile.

Viola, 30-ton side-wheeler built in 1855; 200-bale capacity.

Virginia (No. 1), 141-ton stern-wheeler built in 1860; 631-bale capacity; Pickensville trade 1863–64 season; Columbus trade 1865–66 season; in 1867, it transported cotton to Mobile (probably from Moore's Bluff) for James Sykes of Columbus; freight charge was five dollars per bale; it was snagged at Claiborne, Alabama, 9/11/1869.

Virginia No. 2, 228-ton side-wheeler built in 1864; 506-bale capacity or higher; burned at Tombigbee River, 3/1/1868.

Wabash, 118-ton side-wheeler built in 1827; 676-bale capacity; burned 12/10/1836.

Warrior, 378-ton side-wheeler built in 1857; sparks from its passing probably caused the fire on the *Eliza Battle* 3/1/1858; Columbus trip in April 1863; Vienna trade, February 1862; Pickensville trade, September 1863; abandoned 1872.

Wave, 78-ton side-wheeler built in 1844; in 1848, made record time of fifty-eight hours from Mobile to Aberdeen; stranded at St. James, Louisiana, 3/7/1849.

Waverly, built circa 1845; 827-bale capacity; Upper Tombigbee trade in 1845.

Waverly, built circa 1859; 2,223-bale capacity or higher; Upper Tombigbee trade 1859–61 and 1866.

W.F. Bethea, 242-ton stern-wheeler built in 1902; the steamer sank in laidup fleet, Bayou Sara, circa 1914.

W.H. Gardner, 174-ton stern-wheeler built in 1880; it was 150 feet long and 28 feet wide; Columbus trade, 1880s; burned at Howard's Bar, three miles below Gainesville, Alabama, 3/1/1887; twenty-two lives lost, including a Mr. Blackman of Columbus, Mississippi, as well as 500 bales of cotton from the Columbus Compress Company; it was going from Columbus to Mobile.

Wilcox, 260-ton side-wheeler built in 1851; 1,861-bale capacity; Saturday packet Mobile-Columbus-Waverly, 1853; Plymouth packet, 1853–54; it grounded at Ten Mile Shoals in 1854; may have salvaged engines from hull of *Eliza Battle* in 1858 at Kemp's Landing; abandoned 1858.

The steamer *Wave*.

Wild Cat, 45-ton built in 1829; Columbus trade, 1831; exploded at Demopolis 1/15/1832, one life lost.

William Bradstreet, 247-ton side-wheeler built in 1845; 1,331-bale capacity; snagged at Lackey's Ferry, near Aberdeen, Mississippi, 3/1852.

William Hulbert, 107-ton side-wheeler built in 1836; 345-bale capacity or higher; Mobile-Columbus trade, spring 1839; burned five miles above Mobile, Alabama, 7/26/1839; the fire was discovered while the passengers were at the supper table; there were about thirty-five passengers on board; two lives were lost.

William R. King, 233-ton side-wheeler built in 1845; 1,481-bale capacity or higher; Thursday packet Mobile-Columbus in 1845–46; in November 1845, advertised as "new, and built in expressly for the above trade [Columbus]. Scheduled to leave Mobile at 5 PM Thursday, arrive Columbus Saturday at 8 PM, and return to Mobile Wednesday morning at 8." Collided with Winona, Tombigbee River 2/5/1847, and sank with two lives were lost.

William S. Barry, 275-ton side-wheeler built in 1859; 1,412-bale capacity; it was the weekly Pickensville and Union Bluff packet in 1860 and in the Aberdeen trade 1862; made one trip to Columbus during 1862–63 season

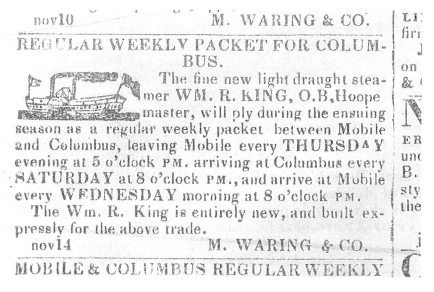

nov10 M. WARING & CO.

REGULAR WEEKLY PACKET FOR COLUM-
BUS.

The fine new light draught steamer WM. R. KING, O.B.Hoope
master, will ply during the ensuing
season as a regular weekly packet between Mobile
and Columbus, leaving Mobile every THURSDAY
evening at 5 o'clock PM. arriving at Columbus every
SATURDAY at 8 o'clock PM., and arrive at Mobile
every WEDNESDAY morning at 8 o'clock PM.

The Wm. R. King is entirely new, and built expressly for the above trade.

nov14 M. WARING & CO.

MOBILE & COLUMBUS REGULAR WEEKLY

An 1845 advertisement from the *Mobile Register* for the steamer *Wm. R. King*.

but was captured in 1864; after the war, it was sold and renamed *Admiral* in 1865; abandoned 1872.

William S. Holt, 225-ton stern-wheeler built in 1875 and sold to Tombigbee interest to run between Columbus and railroad at Demopolis that connected to Savannah, Georgia; Columbus, Mississippi interest and the Central Railroad and Banking Company of Georgia jointly owned it; 135 feet by 28 feet, and its lightest draught was 16 inches; its cabin could accommodate thirty passengers, and it could carry 700 to 800 bales of cotton; the size of its boiler was 22 feet long and 42 inches in diameter; it had two 10-inch cylinders with 4.5 foot strike pistons and two forty-horsepower engines; in dead water, its top speed was twelve miles per hour; it was in the Upper Tombigbee trade in 1875 through 1879; in 1877, it was the regular Tuesday Pickensville-Mobile packet.

William T. Barry, 148-ton side-wheeler built in 1832; 426-bale capacity or higher; Mobile packet in April 1834; there was a lawsuit over lost cargo in Columbus in the Lowndes County Circuit Court in case no. 62-2; stranded at Lake Ponchartrain, Louisiana, 3/19/1836.

William W. Fry, 303-ton side-wheeler built in 1840; 1,703-bale capacity or higher; hull was 180 feet by 28 feet by 8 feet; first iron hull on Tombigbee; abandoned 1858.

Winona, 135-ton side-wheeler built in 1845; 808-bale capacity or higher; collision with *Wm. R. King* on the Tombigbee 2/5/1847; *King* sank and two died; snagged at Warrior River, 5/7/1847.

Wonder, keelboat; in the Columbus-Mobile trade in 1849.

Yazoo, 150-ton side-wheeler built in 1834; 629-bale capacity or higher; abandoned 1845.

Yazoo City, 229-ton side-wheeler built in 1843; 1,059-bale capacity or higher; snagged at Commerce, Mississippi, 1848.

Young Renown, steamer salvaged 178 bales of cotton from the wreck of the Martin's Bluff flatboat *Quincy* in 1848.

UNNAMED boat, built in 1816 when Richard Breckenridge came overland from Tennessee to the site where Columbus would be built; there he built boats for his family to travel downriver to what became Marengo County, Alabama.

UNNAMED flatboat, 12-ton burthen "with oars and cable"; built in March 1814 by Samuel Davis for George Gaines at John Pitchlynn's at the mouth of Tibbee to transport Choctaw Factory supplies to St. Stephens.

UNNAMED keelboat; Gibbs: "Thomas Sampson came to this place [Columbus, Mississippi] in the summer of 1817, and his father-in-law, Esq. Silas McBee, who was to follow him the ensuing fall. He brought with him two Negro men and after building his cabin he proceeded to build a small Keel-boat, which he and the Negroes took down the river to Mobile, and brought it back loaded with family supplies and a small cargo of salt, for sale when purchasers came. He deposited his salt in a little cabin which he built in after his return from Mobile." It was probably in 1819 when Sampson actually built the keelboat.

UNNAMED keelboat, Columbus-Mobile trade about 1819; Ovid P. Brown, captain; salt and sugar were among the supplies transported to Columbus.

UNNAMED keelboat, owned by a Caldwell of Tuscaloosa; arrived at Columbus in 1819 with a cargo of "Indian goods"; Gideon Lincecum purchased the boat and cargo and hired the "boat hands"; he sent the boat back to Mobile to obtain a cargo of sugar, coffee and whiskey to sell in Columbus.

UNNAMED keelboat, brought supplies up Tibbee Creek to the Mayhew Mission in 1822.

Compiled from publications by Bert Neville, John E. Rodabough, J.H. Scruggs Jr., W.A. Evan; W.E. Gibbs, Ward Kaye and Lloyd Neault; from Monroe County, Alabama Heritage Museum; from Columbus, Mississippi and Mobile, Alabama newspapers; from the Waterways Journal; from Billups-Garth Archives of the Columbus-Lowndes Public Library in Columbus, Mississippi; from Bryan Public Library in West Point, Mississippi; and from Special Collections at Mitchell Memorial Library, Mississippi State University.

APPENDIX 5

IMPORTANT LANDINGS ON THE LITTLE TOMBIGBEE

Important Alabama landings in 1879 on the "Little Tombigbee" River included:

Demopolis, mile 242; Forkland, 260; Jone's Bluff, 292; Trussel's Ferry, 306; Cherry Bluff, 313; Gainesville, 315; Mouth of Noxubee, 317; Smith's Ferry, 320; China Bluff, 326; Clanton's Bluff, 326; Warsaw, 328; Mouth of Sipsey, 340; Vienna, 343; Cuba, 344; Catfish Bend, 349; Summerville, 359; Stone's Ferry, 360; Fairfield, 361; Memphis, 369; Ringgold's Bluff, 373; Nance's Ferry, 380; Pickensville, 381; Mouth of Cool Fire, 384; and Petty's Bluff, at mile 389, the last landing in Alabama.

The landings that were located in Mississippi in 1879 on the river included:

Blewett's Shed, 390; Nashville, 392; Colbert's, 443; Union Bluff, 393; Barton's Ferry, 443; McCarty's Bluff, 394; Harvery's Bluff, 397; Moore's Bluff, 399; Hairston's, 400; Lindsay's Ferry, 408; Pinhook 409; Cox's W'yd, 412; Erwin's, 413; Butler's, 415; Neal's, 418; Law's, 419; Columbus, Mississippi, 420; Westport, 421; Malone's Cotton S'd, 423; Plymouth Bluff, 426; Barry's, 430; Burt's Gin, 433; Waverly Ferry, 434; Cox's Woodyard, 438; Collin's Woodyard, 440; Parker's Bluff, 444; Barton's, 444; Vinton's Ferry, 445; Hamilton's old, 453; Allen's or Tatum's, 454; Ogburne's, 459; Lowndesville, 408; Gore's, 461; Vera Cruz, 462; Mrs. Dan Willis, 464; Saund'rs' or Tayl's,

China Bluff Landing, Alabama, at mile 326 on the Tombigbee River in 1921.

Plymouth Bluff Landing, Mississippi, at mile 426 on the Tombigbee in 1920.

Waverly Ferry Landing, Mississippi, at mile 434 on the Tombigbee in 1920.

467; Jenkins' Woody'd, 467; Lackay's, 468; N. Whitfields', 469; Strawhorns', 469; Martin's Bluff, 469; Aberdeen, Mississippi, 470; Joe May's, 473; Parrsville, 475; Reynold's Bluff, 476; John Thompson's, 478; Mullen's, 479; and Cotton Gin Port, 480.

This table of landings is taken from the list in Bert Neville's Directory of Steam: Some Motor Towboats and U.S. Engineer Department Vessels on the Mobile-Alabama-Tombigbee-Warrior Rivers *(1881–1947), which cited* Berney's Handbook of Alabama *(1879) as his source.*

Notes

Introduction

1. Toulmin, "Some Account of the Tombigbee Settlement."
2. U.S. Army Corps of Engineers, *Report of the Chief of Engineers*, Appendix K, 1881.
3. Ibid.
4. Marestier, *Memoir on Steamboats*, 60–61.
5. *New York Herald*, October 23, 1811.
6. Frazer, "Early History of Steamboats," 5.

Chapter 1

1. Kaye, Ward Jr. and Neault, *By the Flow of the Inland River*, 107.
2. Romans, *Concise Natural History*, 208.
3. National Archives, "Choctaw Trading House at St. Stephens."
4. Elliott and Wells, *Cotton Gin Port*.
5. Flint, *Recollections of the Last Ten Years*, 14–16.
6. National Archives, "Choctaw Trading House at St. Stephens."
7. Kaye, Ward and Neault, 48; Gaines, "Reminiscences of Early Times." Reprinted in Kaye, A12–A13.
8. Kaye, Ward and Neault.

9. Plaisance, "Choctaw Trading House 1803–1822," 393–423.

10. Breckenridge, *Diary of Richard Breckenridge*, 142.

11. Gibbs, "Columbus in Its Growth and Infancy." Oscar Keeler wrote in 1848 that Thomas Sampson moved to Columbus about June 1819. Gibbs gave a date of late 1817, but Keeler's sources appeared to be people who moved to Columbus in 1819.

12. Brown, "Autobiography of George Reese Brown," 111. Again Keeler said that Ovid Brown moved to Columbus after June 1819. Brown said 1818.

13. Lincecum, *Adventures of a Frontier Naturalist*.

14. Rodabough, *Steamboats on the Upper Tombigbee*.

15. American Board of Commissioners for Foreign Missions, *Missionary Herald for the Year 1822*.

CHAPTER 2

1. Owen, *History of Alabama*.

2. *Paulson's American Daily Advertiser*, March 10, 1819.

3. Owen, *History of Alabama*.

4. Frazer, "Early History of Steamboats," 5.

5. *Mobile Gazette and Commercial Advertiser*, April 26, 1820.

6. Smith, *Journals of Welcome Arnold Greene*, 142.

7. *Halcyon & Tombecbe*, May 26, 1821.

8. Frazer, "Early History of Steamboats."

9. Snedecor, *Directory of Green County*.

10. Ibid.

11. Keeler, *Keeler's Almanac, 1848*.

12. Sarah Neilson Scrapbook.

13. Brown, "Autobiography of George Reese Brown," 111.

14. Shaeffer, "Historical Sketch of Columbus." The history is undated, but Shaeffer, who arrived in Columbus in 1822, had published another article in 1872 titled "Columbus in 1822 by its Oldest Inhabitant." He died in 1886.

15. Hamilton, *Colonial Mobile*, 448.

16. Rodabough, *Steamboats on the Upper Tombigbee*.

17. Brown, "Autobiography of George Reese Brown," 111.

18. Hamilton, *Colonial Mobile*, 472.
19. *Halcyon & Tombecbe*, April 27, 1822.
20. Frazer, "Early History of Steamboats."
21. Neville, *Directory of River Packets*.

CHAPTER 3

1. Frazer, "Early History of Steamboats"; Foster, "Antebellum Floating Palaces."
2. Kane, *Western River Steamboat*, 67.
3. Frazer, "Early History of Steamboats."
4. Kane, *Western River Steamboat*, 70.
5. Ibid., 67.
6. *Every Saturday*, September 2, 1871.
7. Olmsted, *A Journey in the Seaboard and Slave States*, 192.
8. Frazer, "Early History of Steamboats," 23.
9. Wheatley, interview in 1992.
10. Lanman, *Adventures in the Wilds*, 171.

CHAPTER 4

1. Frazer, "Early History of Steamboats."
2. *Every Saturday*, September 2, 1871.
3. Frazer, "Early History of Steamboats."
4. Ibid.; Foster, "Antebellum Floating Palaces."
5. Olmsted, *A Journey in the Seaboard and Slave States*, 209.
6. *Ballou's Pictorial* 13, no. 22.
7. *Ballou's Pictorial* 8, no. 16.
8. Olmsted, cited in Frazer, "Early History of Steamboats," 18, 27.
9. Burkhardt, "Cahaba: Alabama's Early Capital."
10. Frazer, "Early History of Steamboats," 17.
11. Hopkins, Scrapbook entry dated October 8, 1936.
12. Sick, "Steamboat Days in the Alabama Black Belt."
13. Hopkins, Scrapbook entry.

CHAPTER 5

1. *Columbus Primitive Republican*, June 1851.
2. *Columbus Democrat*, February 22, 1851.
3. Hopkins, Scrapbook entry.
4. Frazer, "Early History of Steamboats"; Foster, "Antebellum Floating Palaces."
5. Frazer, "Early History of Steamboats," 21.
6. Baylies, "A Running Account of Matters & Things," in *Dukes County Intelligencer*, vol. 40, no. 4, 227, and vol. 42, no. 1, 4.
7. *Mobile Register and Journal*, March 31, 1846.
8. Columbus newspaper clipping in vertical file, Billups-Garth Archives, Columbus-Lowndes Public Library.
9. *Harper's New Monthly Magazine*, "A Winter in the South."
10. Rodabough, *Steamboats on the Upper Tombigbee*, 14.
11. *Cooper v. Barry.*
12. Lanman, *Adventures in the Wilds.*
13. Columbus newspaper clippings from the *Columbus Whig*, November and December 1843; the *Columbus Southern Standard*, February 12, 1853; and a clipping from an unidentified Columbus newspaper dated 1853 in the Rufus Ward Collection at the Billups-Garth Archives, Columbus-Lowndes Public Library.

CHAPTER 6

1. Wikipedia, "List of ghost ships."
2. Neville, *Directory of River Packets.*
3. *James Blair v. Cox Brainard & Co.*
4. *New York Times*, April 14, 1854.
5. *James Blair v. Cox Brainard & Co.*
6. Ibid.
7. Board of Supervising Inspectors, *Executive Documents*, 268.
8. *Cox Brainard & Co. v. Foscue.*
9. MacKay, *Life and Liberty in America*, 4–5.
10. William Weir Estate.

11. Doster and Weaver, *Tenn-Tom Country*, 4–5. In addition, the residences of both the victims and survivors of the *Eliza Battle* indicate that they would most likely have boarded it at Gainesville, Warsaw, Fairfield, Pickensville and Columbus.

12. Stallworth, "River Tragedy Was Episode in Love Story."

13. Obituary of Augustus Jones, Blair Scrapbook, Billups-Garth Archives: "Augustus Jones left this city some two weeks ago, blooming in health and buoyant with hope—eager to enter upon the grand drama and play his part in the active scenes of life, as all aspiring youths are—he was but twenty-one last April—Mobile was the place of his destination, which he reached in due time. Returning by the railroad, he crossed over to Gainesville, where he got on board the ill fated steamer Eliza Battle. The rest of his story is told in a few words. He was among the lost—frozen to death, and his remains were yesterday brought to this place…His untimely and tragical death has cast a gloom over our little city, and this entire community sincerely and deeply condole with his Aged parents and other relatives in their irreparable loss." The *Gainesville Independent* of Saturday, March 6, 1858, reported that among the lost was Reverend Newman of Pickensville. This was taken from one of the first reports out of Mobile. Newman was actually from Louisville, Kentucky. The early mistake in his place of residence would probably indicate he had boarded the *Eliza Battle* in Pickensville; Clark, Letter to the *Macon Beacon*. Clark served in Company G, Noxubee Cavalry, with Frank Mauldin during the Civil War. Clark wrote that during the war, Mauldin, a survivor of the *Eliza Battle*, would talk about the disaster and about clinging to a tree that he had climbed in order to save himself. He would "get very nervous" in cold weather.

14. Wyatt, *Autobiography of a Little Man*; *Tuskegee Southwestern Baptist*, Tuskegee, Alabama, 3rd issue, March, 1858. This account, written just weeks after the incident, has the steamer leaving Gainesville on Sunday, February 28. It also says that all passengers were asleep when the fire was discovered, as does the *Gainesville Independent* of Saturday, March 13, 1858. The *Gainesville Independent* refers to the *Eliza Battle* having "touched at Gainesville on Sabbath the last day of February."

15. *Gainesville Independent*, March 13, 1858; MacKay, *Life and Liberty in America*.

16. *New Orleans Daily Picayune*, March 5, 1858.

17. *Gainesville Independent*, March 13, 1858; MacKay, *Life and Liberty in America*.

18. Frazer, "Early History of Steamboats," 10, referring to a party going on when the alarm was given; the *Gainesville Independent*, March 13, 1858, reported that the passengers were asleep when the fire was discovered.

19. *New Albany Ledger*, March 11, 1858.

20. *New Orleans Daily Picayune*, March 5, 1858.

21. *Okolona Prairie News*, March 11, 1858.

22. Board of Supervising Inspectors, *Executive Documents*, 268.

23. *New Albany Ledger*, March 11, 1858.

24. *New Orleans Daily Picayune*, March 6, 1858.

25. *New Orleans Daily Picayune*, March 5, 1858.

26. *Gainesville Independent*, March 13, 1858.

27. Spencer, Letter postmarked Memphis, Tennessee, March 26, 1951.

28. *New Orleans Daily Picayune*, March 5, 1858.

29. *New Orleans Daily Picayune*, March 5, 1858.

30. Frazer, "Early History of Steamboats."

31. *New Orleans Daily Picayune*, March 6, 1858.

32. Frazer, "Early History of Steamboats," 10.

33. Wyatt, *Autobiography of a Little Man*.

34. Mrs. Lillie Borden, Letter postmarked Reform, Alabama, March 22, 1951.

35. Medical Association of the State of Alabama, *Alabama Medical Journal*, 259.

36. *New Orleans Daily Picayune*, March 5, 1858.

37. MacKay, *Life and Liberty in America*, 191.

38. *New Orleans Daily Picayune*, March 5, 1858.

39. Personal communication from Mrs. C.R. Friday, West Point, Mississippi, 2000.

40. Mary Ruth Caradine, interview with Jack Elliott, January 12, 1986. Dird C. Caradine (1837–1924) was her grandfather; another account of the *Eliza Battle* is contained in the *WPA Source Materials for Mississippi History, Lowndes County*, compiled by Sadie Hudson. There it is stated that Mr. and Mrs. Allen Blewett were going from Columbus to Mobile on their honeymoon on the *Eliza Battle* and survived. They completed their trip by stagecoach. This oral tradition has a problem in that Blewett family records indicate that Allen Blewett was married in Louisiana on March

NOTES TO PAGES 85–86

12, 1858. The Blewetts may have been on the *Battle*, but if they had been, they were not on their honeymoon.

41. Doster and Weaver, *Tenn-Tom Country*.

42. Wyatt, *Autobiography of a Little Man*.

43. *New Orleans Daily Picayune*, March 5, 1858.

44. *New Orleans Daily Picayune*, March 6, 1858.

45. Glass, *A Goodly Heritage*.

46. Frazer, "Early History of Steamboats."

47. *New York Times*, March 12, 1858.

48. *New Orleans Daily Picayune*, March 5, 1858.

49. On March 12, 1858, the *New York Times* published an account of the "Burning of the Steamer Eliza Battle," which had appeared in the March 4 edition of the *Mobile Advertiser*. The article concluded with a list of those who were lost and included thirty-three persons: "The following is a list of those ascertained to have been lost: Mrs. B. Cromwell and child, frozen, Sumter County; *Mrs.* H.G. Turner and child, frozen, Washington County; Mr. W.T. Smith, frozen, Green County; Mr. Caradine, frozen, Chickasaw County; Mr. Willis, frozen, Chickasaw County; Mr. Agustus Jones, frozen, Columbus, Miss.; Mr. Martin, frozen, Kentucky; Mr. John Powell, barkeeper, frozen, Eliza Battle; Dr. S.W. Clanton, frozen, Warsaw, Ala.; A young man, unknown, frozen, Fairfield, Ala.; Negro man belonging to B.L. Turner, frozen; Negro man, 'Jackson,' barber, frozen, Eliza Battle; Barnett, cook, frozen, Eliza Battle; Nancy, chambermaid, belonging to S.G. Stone, master of the Eliza Battle, frozen; Robert, cabin-boy, belonging to Col. T. Buford; Dick, cabin-boy, belonging to Judge R. C. Torrey; Jim, cabin-boy, belonging to Jno. Foster; White boy, (third cook), name unknown; Sam, Peter and Jack, deck hands, belonging to J.A. Mooring; Bill, deck hand, belonging to R.G. McMahon; Allen, deck hand, belonging to John Bowen; Ben, deck hand, belonging to Dan Raine; Rev. Mr. Newman, frozen, from Louisville, Ky.; M.A. Galloway, never seen, Gainesville, Ala.; Three white deck hands, never seen; P. Kirkland, died after getting ashore, Greene Co., Ala.; Mrs. Cromwell and her child, died from cold, in her husband's arms, in a tree; Dr. S.H. Jones, never seen, Greene Co. Ala.; The bodies were not recovered of the following: Dr. S.H. Jones, M.A. Galloway, Rev. Mr. Newman, white boy, 3rd cook; Jack, negro; Bill, negro; three white deck hands, chambermaid." The *Times*

article was picked up by the *Nelson Examiner and New Zealand Chronicle*, July 7, 1858, page 3, which reported: "Particulars of the destruction of the steamer Eliza Battle by fire, near Demopolis, are published by the New York papers. The wind was very high at the time, and almost as soon as discovered the fire communicated to the ladies 1 cabin, and cut off access to the lifeboat and yawl. All on board were driven forward, where they remained until the flames drove them into the water. The boat was headed for the shore, but the river being high and over its banks, and the wheel-ropes burnt, a landing could not be effected. There were from 50 to 60 passengers on board, and the number lost was by one account 29, and by another 33. A majority of them were frozen. The steamer was driven among the trees, where she lodged until the engines ceased to work, and the passengers sought safety by clinging to the limbs and branches of trees, and to bales of cotton thrown overboard. The fire had its origin among the cotton on the after deck, under the ladies' cabin; it could not be accounted for, unless it was from sparks from the steamer Warrior, which passed to windward about half-an-hour before the fire was discovered."

50. McDonald, *History of the Cumberland Presbyterian Church*. Newman probably boarded the *Battle* at Pickensville, as the list of those lost published in the *Gainesville Independent* on March 6, 1858, identified him as from Pickensville rather than his actual residence in Kentucky.
51. *Evening Picayune*, New Orleans, March 5, 1858.
52. *Gainesville Independent*, March 6, 1858.
53. Board of Supervising Inspectors, *Executive Documents*, 268.
54. Carlisle, personal communication, December 17, 2003.
55. MacKay, *Life and Liberty in America*.
56. From Belloc, *A Passing World*: "My next anecdote is widely different. An intimate friend of my own, a woman known to all her generation, a friend of John Stuart Mill and of the whole range of intellectual and free-thinking England forty years ago, was traveling with her husband in America. Of the two he was the more inclined to mysticism, though by profession he belonged to one of the most positive of sciences. They were at St Louis, and were proposing to take a boat for New Orleans, the said boat bearing the odd name of the Eliza Battle. The arrangements had been made by the husband, and were all complete. But in the night,

my clear-headed friend, who scoffed at every kind of superstition, got a sudden and utterly causeless objection to the steamer. She went to the quay with her husband, saying, 'I will not go by the Eliza Battle.' He was much upset, saying she was a good boat, and a manuscript respectable boat, and it was all settled; and how could she be so foolishly unlike her sensible self. She was driven to bay, and had no defense, but simply said, 'No, I will not go by the Eliza Battle'; and, of course, her husband, grumbling much, had to give in. The Eliza Battle never reached New Orleans. She went down on a 'snag'—one of those uprooted trees which used to be, and perhaps still are, the great danger of the Mississippi. My friend used to tell this story, with half-laughing scorn of her own solitary bit of willful superstition, which, nevertheless, saved both their lives."

57. William Weir Estate; Doster and Weaver, *Tenn-Tom Country*, 5.
58. Dickson, "Burning of the 'Eliza Battle,'" *Birmingham Age-Herald*. Typed manuscript found among the papers of Elizabeth Garth Vestal Daniel, who was a feature writer for the *Birmingham News*.
59. Carlisle, personal communication, December 17, 2003.

Chapter 7

1. Rodabough, *Steamboats on the Upper Tombigbee*, 57.
2. Ibid.
3. Kane, *Western River Steamboat*, 34–35.
4. Auken, *Portrait and Biographical Album of Jackson County*.
5. Cate, *Two Soldiers*.
6. Bentley, *History of the 77th Illinois*.
7. Foster, "Antebellum Floating Palaces," 18.
8. Ibid, 19.
9. Ibid.
10. *Mobile Advertiser and Register*, January 22, 1863.
11. Foster, "Antebellum Floating Palaces," 18.
12. U.S. Naval War Records Office, *Official Records of the Union and Confederate Navies*.
13. Secretary of State, Illinois, *Regimental and Unit Histories*.
14. Neville, *Directory of River Packets*.

Chapter 8

1. *Columbus Press*, January 24, 1874, and January 30, 1875.
2. *West Alabamian*, March 3, 1875.
3. Janes, *Hand-Book of the State of Georgia*, 173.
4. W.H. Hargrove Estate.
5. Janes, *Hand-Book of the State of Georgia*.
6. U.S. Army Corps of Engineers, *Report of the Chief of Engineers*, Appendix K, 1882, 1,287–1,298.
7. Ibid., 1,287.
8. Ibid., 1,289.
9. Ibid., 1,291.
10. Ibid., 1,289.
11. Ibid., 1,290.
12. U.S. Army Corps of Engineers, *Report of the Chief of Engineers*, Appendix B, 1890.
13. Columbus newspaper clipping, 1875, Steamboat Vertical File, Billups-Garth Archives, Columbus-Lowndes Public Library.
14. U.S. Army Corps of Engineers, *Report of the Chief of Engineers*, Appendix K, 1881.
15. Ibid.
16. Watson, interview.

Chapter 9

1. Hodnett, *Once Upon a Place*.
2. Doster and Weaver, *Tenn-Tom Country*.
3. Ibid., Map 14.
4. *Vienna Landing Ledger 1898–1902*, Billups-Garth Archives, Columbus-Lowndes Public Library.
5. Ibid.
6. Ibid.
7. U.S. Army Corps of Engineers, *Report of the Chief of Engineers, U.S. Army, Tombigbee River (1916)*.

Chapter 10

1. Manager, Alabama Cotton Oil Company, Demopolis, Alabama, to J.W. Gentry, Warsaw, Alabama, May 8, 1906.
2. Neville, Letter dated April 19, 1958.
3. *Columbus Dispatch*, January 25, 1906.
4. "The American Burned at Mobile in 1915."
5. *Waterways Journal* 21, no. 21.
6. *Columbus Weekly Dispatch.*
7. *Waterways Journal; Columbus Commercial*, February 21, 1909.
8. *Columbus Dispatch*, December 31, 1908.
9. *Waterways Journal* 21, no. 21.
10. *Columbus Commercial*, January 12, 1913.
11. Neville, *Directory of River Packets.*
12. Neville, *Directory of Steam.*
13. *Report of the Chief of Engineers, U.S. Army, Annual Reports of the War Department*, 1914.
14. Ibid., for the years 1890, 1892, 1907, 1909, 1914, 1919.
15. *Report of the Chief of Engineers, U.S. Army, Annual Reports of the War Department*, 1914.
16. Chief of Engineers, U.S. Army, *Tombigbee River from Demopolis…*, 64th Cong. 1st sess., House Documents Vol. 24, May 17, 1916, 8.
17. Duryea, "Commercial Cars in Popular Use," *New York Times*, January 9, 1911.

BIBLIOGRAPHY

American Board of Commissioners for Foreign Missions. *Missionary Herald for the Year 1822*. Vol. 18. Boston: self-published, 1822.

"The American Burned at Mobile in 1915." Undated newspaper clipping from unknown newspaper. Located in the files of the Tennessee-Tombigbee Waterway Transportation Museum, Columbus, Mississippi.

Auken, Hilda Van. *Portrait and Biographical Album of Jackson County, Michigan.* N.p.: Chapman Brothers, 1890.

Ballou's Pictorial 8, no. 16 (April 21, 1855).

Ballou's Pictorial 13, no. 22 (November 28, 1857).

Baylies, Henry. "A Running Account of Matters & Things." *Dukes County Intelligencer*, vol. 40, no. 4, 1999, page 227, and vol. 42, no. 1, 2000, page 4. Located at the Dukes County Historical Society in Edgartown, Massachusetts.

Belloc, Bessie Rayner. *A Passing World.* London: Ward & Downey Limited, 1897.

Bentley, William H. *History of the 77ᵗʰ Illinois Volunteer Infantry.* N.p., 1883. Digitized webpage version at http://77illinois.homestead.com/files/77il/77ch19.html.

Board of Supervising Inspectors. *Executive Documents, U.S. Senate, Second Session of the 35ᵗʰ Congress, 1858–1859.* Washington, D.C.: Government Printing Office, 1859.

Borden, Mrs Lillie. Letter postmarked "Reform, Alabama, March 22, 1951," a copy of which is in the Bryan Public Library, Local History File, West Point, Mississippi.

Brannon, Peter A., ed. *The Southwestern Baptist.* 3ʳᵈ issue. Tuskegee, AL, March 1858. Reprinted in the *Montgomery Advertiser,* "Through the Years," September 27, 1942.

Breckenridge, Richard. *Diary of Richard Breckenridge.* Edited by H.S. Halbert. Transactions of the Alabama Historical Society 1898–99. Tuscaloosa: Alabama Historical Society, 1899.

Brown, George Reese. "Autobiography of George Reese Brown." Excerpt in Vaughn, Estelle Rogers, ed. *Southern Born and Bred.* Chicago: Adams Press, 1972.

Burkhardt, E. Walter. "Cahaba: Alabama's Early Capital." In Neville, Bert, ed. *A Glance at Old Cahawba, Alabama's Early Capital.* Selma, AL: Selma Printing Service, 1967.

Caradine, Mary Ruth. Interview with Jack Elliott, West Point, Mississippi, January 12, 1986.

Carlisle, William. Personal communication, December 17, 2003.

Cate, Writ Armistead, ed. *Two Soldiers: The Campaign Diaries of Thomas J. Key, CSA and Robert J. Campbell U.S.A.* Chapel Hill: University of North Carolina Press, 1938.

Chief of Engineers, U.S. Army. *Tombigbee River from Demopolis, Ala. to Columbus, Miss.* 64th Cong., 1st sess., House Documents Vol. 24, May 17, 1916.

Clark, M.J. Letter to the *Macon Beacon* dated July 23, 1919, which was published in the *Beacon* on September 29, 1933.

Columbus (MS) Commercial. February 21, 1909.

———. January 12, 1913.

Columbus (MS) Democrat. February 22, 1851.

Columbus (MS) Dispatch. December 31, 1908.

———. January 25, 1906.

Columbus (MS) Press. January 30, 1875.

———. January 24, 1874.

Columbus (MS) Primitive Republican. June 1851. Rufus Ward Collection, Billups-Garth Archives, Columbus-Lowndes Public Library.

Cooper v. Barry. Case no. 3780 of the Lowndes County, Mississippi Circuit Court.

Cox Brainard & Co. v. Foscue. 83 Alabama 709. Alabama Superior Court, 1864. A rehearing of a case appealed from the Mobile City Court in 1859.

Daily (LA) Picayune. March 5, 1858.

———. March 6, 1858.

Dickson, Ella Bacon. "Burning of the 'Eliza Battle' on the Tombigbee River in 1857." *Birmingham Age-Herald.* Typed manuscript in possession of author.

Doster, James, and David C. Weaver. *Tenn-Tom Country: The Upper Tombigbee Valley.* Tuscaloosa: University of Alabama Press, 1997.

Duryea, Charles E. "Commercial Cars in Popular Use." *New York Times,* January 9, 1911.

Elliott, Jack D., Jr., and Mary Ann Wells. *Cotton Gin Port.* Jackson: Mississippi Historical Society, 2003.

Evening (LA) Picayune. March 5, 1858.

Every Saturday. Vol. 3, no. 88, September 2, 1871.

Flint, Timothy. *Recollections of the Last Ten Years.* Boston, 1826. Reprinted, New York: Alfred A. Knopf, 1932.

Foster, Judge Fleetwood. "Antebellum Floating Palaces of the Alabama River." *Wilcox Banner,* 1904. Reprinted and edited by Bert Neville in book form, Selma, Alabama, 1971.

Frazer, Mell A. "Early History of Steamboats in Alabama." Alabama Polytechnic Institute Historical Studies. Third Series. Auburn: Alabama Polytechnic Institute Historical Studies, 1907.

Friday, Mrs. C.R. Personal communication, West Point, Mississippi, 2000.

Gaines, George S., Colonel. "Reminiscences of Early Times in the Mississippi Territory." Five-part series in the *Mobile Register,* June–July 1872. Reprinted in *By the Flow of the Inland River: The Settlement of Columbus, Mississippi to 1825,* cited here.

Gainesville (AL) Independent. March 6, 1858.

———. March 13, 1858.

Gibbs W.E. "Columbus in Its Growth and Infancy." Eight-part series in the *Columbus Index*, 1872.

Glass, Mary Morgan, ed. *A Goodly Heritage: Memories of Green County.* Eutaw, AL: Green County Historical Society, 1977.

Halcyon & Tombecbe. April 27, 1822.

———. May 26, 1821.

Hamilton, Peter J. *Colonial Mobile.* Tuscaloosa: University of Alabama Press, 1976.

Harper's New Monthly Magazine 18, no. 103. "A Winter in the South" (December 1858).

Hodnett, David. *Once Upon a Place: A History of Vienna, Alabama.* Privately published, 2003.

Hopkins, E.R. Scrapbook entry dated October 8, 1936, Billups-Garth Archives, Columbus-Lowndes Public Library, Columbus, Mississippi.

Hudson, Sadie. *WPA Source Materials for Mississippi History, Lowndes County.* Compiled 1936–38. Billups-Garth Archives, Columbus-Lowndes Public Library, Columbus, Mississippi.

James Blair v. Cox Brainard & Co. Circuit Court of Lowndes County, Mississippi. Case no. 9480. Located in the Billups-Garth Archives, Columbus-Lowndes Public Library, Columbus, Mississippi.

Janes, Thomas P. *Hand-Book of the State of Georgia.* Atlanta, GA: Commissioner of Agriculture, 1876.

Kane, Adam I. *The Western River Steamboat.* College Station: Texas A&M University Press, 2004.

Kaye, Samuel H., Rufus Ward Jr. and Carolyn B. Neault. *By the Flow of the Inland River: The Settlement of Columbus, Mississippi to 1825*. Columbus, MS: Snapping Turtle Press, 1992.

Keeler, Oscar, ed. *Keeler's Almanac, 1848*. Billups-Garth Archives, Columbus-Lowndes Public Library, Columbus, Mississippi.

Lanman, Charles. *Adventures in the Wilds of the United States*, Philadelphia, PA: John W. Moore, 1856.

Lardner, Dionysius. *Steam and Its Uses*. London: Walton and Maberly, 1856. Reprinted by Lindsay Publications, 1995.

Lincecum, Gideon. *Adventures of a Frontier Naturalist: The Life and Times of Dr. Gideon Lincecum*. Edited by Jerry Bryan and Edward Hale Phillips. College Station: Texas A&M University Press, 1994.

MacKay, Charles. *Life and Liberty in America*. New York: Harper and Brothers, Publishers, 1859.

Manager, Alabama Cotton Oil Company, Demopolis, Alabama, to J.W. Gentry, Warsaw, Alabama. Letter dated May 8, 1906. Photocopy of letter.

Marestier, Jean Baptiste. *Memoir on Steamboats of the United States of America*. Translated by Sidney Withington. Paris: Royal Press, 1824. Reprinted Mystic, CT: Marine Historical Association, Inc, 1957.

McDonald, Benjamin. *History of the Cumberland Presbyterian Church*. Nashville, TN: Board of Publications of the Cumberland Presbyterian Church, 1899.

Medical Association of the State of Alabama. *Alabama Medical Journal* (1907): 259.

Mobile Advertiser and Register. January 22, 1863.

Mobile Daily Advertiser. March 4, 1858.

Mobile Gazette and Commercial Advertiser. April 26, 1820.

Mobile Register and Journal. March 31, 1846.

National Archives, comp. "Choctaw Trading House at St. Stephens," 1803–1820, Microfilm copy at Mississippi Department of Archives and History, Jackson, Mississippi.

Neville, Bert. *Directory of River Packets in the Mobile-Alabama-Warrior-Tombigbee Trades (1818–1932).* Selma, AL: self-published, 1962.

———. *Directory of Steam: Some Motor-Towboats and U.S. Engineer Department Vessels on the Mobile-Alabama-Tombigbee-Warrior River (1881–1947).* Selma, AL: self-published, 1964.

———. *Directory of Steamboats on the Chattachoochee–Apalachicola River System.* Selma, AL: self-published, 1961.

———. *A Glance at Old Cahawba: Alabama's Early Capital.* Selma, AL: self-published, 1967.

New Albany (IN) Ledger. March 11, 1858.

New York Herald. October 23, 1811.

New York Times. March 12, 1858.

Obituary of Augustus Jones. Newspaper clipping, page 107, in the scrapbook of Elizabeth W. Blair, 1819–1902. Billups-Garth Archives, Columbus-Lowndes Public Library, Columbus, Mississippi.

Okolona (MS) Prairie News. March 11, 1858.

Olmsted, F. Law. *A Journey in the Seaboard and Slave States, with Remarks on their Economy.* New York: Dix and Edwards, 1856.

Owen, Thomas McAdory. *History of Alabama and Dictionary of Alabama Biography.* N.p.: S.J. Clarke Publishing Company, 1921.

Paulson's American Daily Advertiser. March 10, 1819.

Petsche, Jerome E. *The Steamboat Bertrand.* Washington, D.C.: National Park Service, U. S, Department of the Interior, 1974.

Plaisance, Aloysius, Father. "The Choctaw Trading House 1803–1822." *Alabama Historical Quarterly* 16 (Fall–Winter 1954): 393–423.

Rodabough, John E. *Steamboats on the Upper Tombigbee.* Hamilton, MS: Tombigbee Press, 1985.

Romans, Bernard. *A Concise Natural History of East and West Florida.* New York, 1775. Reprinted, New Orleans, LA: Pelican Publishing Company, 1961.

Sarah Neilson Scrapbook. Billups-Garth Archives, Columbus-Lowndes Public Library, Columbus, Mississippi.

Secretary of State, Illinois. *Regimental and Unit Histories.* 1861–1866. www.sos. state.il.us/departments/archives/reghist.pdf.

Shaeffer, George, Reverend. "Historical Sketch of Columbus." In Captain E.T. Sykes Scrapbook. Vol. 1. Billups-Garth Archives, Columbus-Lowndes Public Library, Columbus, Mississippi.

Sick, Glenn N. "Steamboat Days in the Alabama Black Belt, 1875–1917." *Steamboat Bill of Facts*, no. 57 (March 1956).

Smith, Alice E., ed. *The Journals of Welcome Arnold Greene: Journeys in the South 1822–1824.* Madison: State Historical Society of Wisconsin, 1957.

Snedecor, Gayle. *A Directory of Green County for 1855–56.* Mobile, AL, 1856.

Spencer, W.G. Letter postmarked Memphis, Tennessee, March 26, 1951. A copy is located in the Local History File at the Bryan Public Library, West Point, Mississippi.

Stallworth, Clark. "River Tragedy Was Episode in Love Story." *Birmingham News*, March 9, 1975.

Sumpter County Whig. "Eliza Battle is Entirely New." January 4, 1853.

Toulmin, Harry. "Some Account of the Tombigbee Settlement." *United States Gazette*, October 25, 1805.

Tuskegee (AL) Southwestern Baptist. 3rd issue, March 1858. Reprinted in Brannon, Peter A. "Through the Years." *Montgomery Advertiser*, September 27, 1942.

United States Army Corps of Engineers. *Report of the Chief of Engineers.* Appendix B. U.S. Army. Washington, D.C.: Government Printing Office, 1890.

———. *Report of the Chief of Engineers.* Appendix K. U.S. Army. Washington, D.C.: Government Printing Office, 1881.

———. *Report of the Chief of Engineers.* Appendix K. U.S. Army. Washington, D.C.: Government Printing Office, 1882.

———. *Report of the Chief of Engineers, U.S. Army, Annual Reports of the War Department.* Washington, D.C.: Government Printing Office, 1890, 1892, 1907, 1909, 1914 and 1919.

———. *Report of the Chief of Engineers, U.S. Army, Tombigbee River from Demopolis, Ala. To Columbus, Miss.* Washington, D.C.: Government Printing Office, 1916.

U.S. House of Representatives. *Executive Documents, First Session of the 34th Congress, 1855–1856.* Washington, D.C. U.S. Printing Office, 1856.

U.S. Naval War Records Office. *Official Records of the Union and Confederate Navies in the War of the Rebellion.* 1903. United States Office of Naval Records and Library, National Archives and Records Administration. College Park, MD.

Vienna Landing Ledger 1898–1902. Billups-Garth Archives, Columbus-Lowndes Public Library, Columbus, Mississippi.

Waterways Journal 21, no. 21. (August 22, 1908).

Watson, Ethel Smith. Interview in *Tombigbee Historic Town Sites Project Oral History.* Michigan State University, 1980. Copy located in Billups-Garth Archives, Columbus-Lowndes Public Library, Columbus, Mississippi.

West Alabamian. March 3, 1875.

Wheatley, Auther James. Interview in Culpepper, Illinois, 1992. *Life on the Tombigbee Oral History Project.* Edited by T.M. Privately published, n.d.

W.H. Hargrove Estate. Chancery Court of Lowndes County, Mississippi. Billups-Garth Archives, Columbus-Lowndes Public Library, Columbus, Mississippi.

Wikipedia. "List of ghost ships." http://en.wikipedia.org/wiki/List_of_ghost_ships.

William Weir Estate. Probate Court of Lowndes County, Mississippi. Case no. 765. Billups-Garth Archives, Columbus-Lowndes Public Library, Columbus, Mississippi.

Wyatt, R.R. *Autobiography of a Little Man.* Macon, MS: Beacon Office, 1939.

ABOUT THE AUTHOR

Rufus Ward has been active in the fields of history and historic preservation for more than thirty-five years. He divides his time between lectures on history-related topics and consulting on cultural projects. He also writes a weekly history column for the *Commercial Dispatch* in Columbus, Mississippi.

Ward has been a contributing author for two other books: *After Removal: The Choctaw in Mississippi* and *By the Flow of the Inland River: A History of Columbus, Mississippi, to 1825*. Additionally, he has published numerous journal and magazine articles on southern history. He is an advisor emeritus to the National Trust for Historic Preservation, having previously represented the state of Mississippi on its board of advisors.

Birney Imes/ Commercial Dispatch.

Ward's past honors include the Calvin Brown Award from the Mississippi Association of Professional Archaeologists "in recognition of service by an amateur archaeologist in aid of historic preservation in the

State of Mississippi" and a Resolution of Commendation from the board
of trustees of the Mississippi Department of Archives & History for his
"contributions and commitment to the preservation and interpretation of
Mississippi History."

Rufus, a retired prosecuting attorney, resides in a Victorian home in
West Point, Mississippi, with his wife Karen and bird dog Eliza Faye. He
graduated from the University of Mississippi, where he received a BA and a
Juris Doctor. His daughter, Sarah, lives in Alexandria, Virginia, and his son,
Bailey, lives in Bay St. Louis, Mississippi.